THE AGATHA CHRISTIE CROSSWORD PUZZLE BOOK

Compiled by
Randall Toye and Judith Hawkins Gaffney

WINGS BOOKS
New York • Avenel, New Jersey

This 1995 edition is published by Wings Books,
distributed by Random House Value Publishing, Inc.,
40 Engelhard Avenue, Avenel, New Jersey 07001,
by arrangement with Henry Holt and Company, Inc.

Random House
New York • Toronto • London • Sydney • Auckland

Printed and bound in the United States of America

ISBN 0-517-12337-1

8 7 6 5 4 3 2

Contents

OTHER PUZZLES

ANSWERS

Introduction

In bringing together the work of Agatha Christie — the world's most popular mystery author — and the crossword puzzle — which has been referred to as the world's most popular pastime — we have attempted to provide devotees of both Miss Christie and the crossword with an intriguing and demanding entertainment.

The following 44 puzzles are broadly divided into 3 types. The first 20 puzzles are of the standard American style crossword puzzle, with keyed grids and, with the exception of the Christie-related clues, clues of the straight definition type. These clues are apt to point to unusual meanings of common words or to common meanings of more esoteric words. For example, the word "secrete" may be derived from either of the clues "give out" or "hide away," while the clue "wooden plug" may yield the answer "stud" or "labret."

The next 16 puzzles are of the British crossword variety, with unkeyed grids and, with the exception of the Christie-related clues, clues of the cryptic variety. The cryptic clue usually contains 2 parts: a definition or description indicating what the answer *is*, and a secondary clue giving some information *about* the answer. These clues may range from the simple hidden word and the multiple definition form to the more complex anagram within a word and the clue that merely provides the sound of the answer. The clue "piece of furniture in Barnstable's house," for example, is a hidden word clue, which yields the answer "table" (you are looking for a "piece of furniture" within the words "Barnstable's house"), whereas the clue "reveal hideaway" is a multiple definition clue, which yields the answer "secrete."

In each of the American and British style crosswords the Agatha Christie clues are derived from a single Christie book. We have made every attempt to be honest in our selection of clues, avoiding trickery or wording that might confuse you, yet making the clues specific enough to require a careful reading of the books involved and to demand full concentration of your detective powers. The answers are drawn from many areas within the stories, including names and descriptions of characters, places and things — such as victims and witnesses, houses and villages, and murder weapons and jewels.

The last group of 8 puzzles consists of a Title Hunt, 2 Word Finds, a Cipher, a Kriss-Kross, a Word Grid and Match-Up, a Quotefall, and a Double Crostic. With the exception of The Agatha Christie Title Hunt, and The Poisoner's Word Grid and Match-Up, each of the puzzles is again tied to a particular Christie book or a collection of short stories. Instructions for working out these puzzles are provided with each puzzle separately. Complete answers for all 44 puzzles are given at the end of the book.

We hope that this book will bring a new dimension to both your enjoyment of Agatha Christie and your love of the puzzle, and we wish you good solving.

R.T. & J.H.G.

Note: Agatha Christie clues are indicated by an asterisk.

Murder on the Orient Express

ACROSS

* 1 It was embroidered with dragons: 2 wds.
12 London gallery
*13 Daisy Armstrong's sheep-faced nurse
14 Log hut: Russian
17 Black
18 South American wildcats
19 Pentagram
*20 Linda Arden's alias
22 _____ Ziegfeld
23 Birthplace of Chang and Eng
24 One: German
*26 Arbuthnot: the Colonel from _____
28 Market town: French
31 Grassland
*33 Hardman's initials
34 Medially in Oriental supplication
35 United Arab Republic: abbrev.
*36 Daisy's aunt
39 Victor Frankenstein's factotum
41 Ruck
43 Algonquin deity

45 Listen
*46 Western terminus of Orient Express
50 Sycophant
51 In the year of our Lord: abbrev; paid insert
*52 Ford auto salesman's initials
54 A _____ broom sweeps clean
55 Brood
*57 King's _____ ; Poirot retired here in The Murder of Roger Ackroyd
59 Vietnamese neighbor
61 German river
63 Adam's _____
65 Obstruct
69 Threshold
70 Waters
72 Rule: Latin
73 Asiatic weight
74 Part of armor; facet of gem
75 To sign, seal: obs.
*76 She played Hildegard Schmidt in 1974 movie version: 2 wds.

DOWN

1 Stop
2 Workbasket
3 One that does: suffix
4 Lessee
5 Ancient sea
6 _____ your hand
7 Width of cut; to carve
* 8 M. Bouc's suspect choice
9 Perry _____
*10 One of Colonel Arbuthnot's destinations
11 Ancient Roman seaport
15 Bleat
*16 Daisy was one
21 _____ and lows
25 45 inches
*27 Count Andrenyi's embassy location
*28 One of the coaches on Orient Express

29 Rowed
30 Component of mammalian urine
32 Electrical Engineer: abbrev.
34 Odin
37 Common Market: abbrev.
38 Mon _____
40 Japanese city
*42 Author of Love's Captive
*44 _____ Like It, Linda Arden hit: 2 wds.
*47 Mr. Ratchett collected _____ tiles
48 The: French
49 Shoemaker's tool
53 Football position: abbrev.
56 Absorb
57 More adept
58 Goosefoot herb
60 Chemical prefix, aspirin, e.g.
62 _____ Fail, Irish crowning stone
64 Found in a China shop

DOWN continued

66 _____ Rabbit
67 Revise
68 Fouls
71 Air

The A.B.C. Murders

ACROSS

* 1 Type of service considered pleasingly symmetrical by Poirot
5 Regarding stop: 2 wds.
10 Dull
13 Without "you"
14 Rhone tributary
15 Danish money
*17 Throat specialist
19 Thatching grass
20 Bitter vetch
21 Act
*22 Jealous murder suspect
24 Three-toed sloth
25 By mouth
*26 How Poirot said he always regarded Captain Hastings
*29 Albert _____ , he wanted Gold Flake
33 Attentive
34 Pilgrimage terminus
36 Stag mate
37 Ready for harvest
38 Australian bird
39 Safecracker
40 Outer: comb. form
41 Belonging to novelist Victor
43 Nimbi of comets
44 Verse form based on six stanzas
46 North American carnivores
47 Ardor
49 Article: French
50 Regarding stars
53 Epochal
*55 _____ ami; one of Poirot's friends
58 Hades' abode
*59 Tea offered at Ginger Cat
*62 Mrs. Fowler's daughter
63 Malayan gum resin
64 Utilizes
65 Rhine tributary
66 Fundamental units of force
67 Solid to liquid

DOWN

* 1 Chief Inspector Japp to Poirot— " _____ fungus sprouting finer than ever"
2 Shakespearian king
3 Graces' mate
* 4 _____ Hartigan, Lily Marbury's friend
* 5 He made arrangements for possible "D" surveillance
6 District in northeastern Surrey, United Kingdom
* 7 Site of "A" murder wound
8 Mineral deposit
9 Anglo-Saxon name
*10 He was told by Betty Barnard she was going to St. Leonards
11 Rages
12 Buddy
*16 Carmichael Clarke's title
*18 Captain Hastings thought he sent first letter
23 Royal Academy of Dramatic Arts, London: abbrev.
24 40 of these and a mule were post-war bonus
25 Roman abode of the dead
*26 Poirot confused them with wasps
27 Chased White Rabbit
28 Ancient Irish tribes
30 Swelling
*31 Lady Clarke's physician
32 Roman laws
*34 Sister of "B," Captain Hastings fell for her
35 Egyptian Monetary Organization: abbrev.
39 Pair
*41 He saw Not a Sparrow at Torquay Pavilion
42 Without help

*43 Chief Inspector Japp to Poirot —
"Pity to let those grey _____
function unnecessarily"
45 She's behind a wicket
*48 Yard man in charge of ABC case
50 Pronoun
51 Berber tribe
52 Lamb's pen name
53 Uniform

54 Fennel of the Philippine Is.
*55 Hampshire constable described
the _____ en scene to Poirot
56 City on Oka in Western Russia
*57 Basis of Poirot's confusion at 26
Down
60 Cathedral city in United
Kingdom
61 Bee noise

Cards on the Table

ACROSS

* 1 The one with money in Wendon Cottage
  6 Colored
*10 Ariadne Oliver's book, *The* _____ *in the Library*
 14 Norse sea god
*15 Mysterious colonel
 16 Nichol's hero
 17 Late Latin: abbrev.
 18 Circle circumference
*19 Mr. Shaitana's possible origin
 21 Professional Golfers' Association: abbrev.
 23 Corrosive
 25 Terrier, e.g.
*26 One of Mr. Shaitana's Persian carpets
 28 Maid
 29 Wayfarer's rest
 30 Musical gymnasts
*33 Service that 15 Across was in
 36 Therefore: Latin
 37 First card
 39 Bitter and stout, e.g.

 40 Hail: Latin
 41 Swedish liquid measure
 42 Clan: Greek
 43 African gazelle
 45 Compliment
*47 Loquacious lady who did for Wendon Cottage
 49 To go: Scottish
 50 Leisure
*51 Poirot's cigarettes
 55 Cat's delight
 58 Pudding base
 59 United Press International: abbrev.
 60 Versatile
 62 Christian era: abbrev.
 64 Page: abbrev.
 65 Oriental intoxicant
 66 Great yell
 67 Russian currency
 69 Adam's loss
 70 Monks
 71 United Kingdom coast

DOWN

* 1 _____ Wood figure, card room ornament
  2 Woman's name
  3 King of Bashan
  4 Plunge in liquid
* 5 Hjerson's creator
* 6 *The Death in the* _____ *Pipe*
* 7 Investigative bureau
  8 Economic Cooperation Group: abbrev.
* 9 Rhoda Dawes's gardening-mad aunt
*10 He always looked misleadingly stupid
 11 Notice of demise
 12 Eat
 13 Time measure
 20 Sleep: comb. form
 22 Exist

 24 Bevel
 27 Vapors
 28 Depot: French
*30 Shaitana exemplar
 31 Branch
*32 What was on Hugh's face
 33 Sea worm
 34 Napoleonic exile
 35 Third letters
 38 Before: arch.
 40 American Medical Laboratory Engineers: abbrev.
 41 American author
 43 Anticipate
*44 He lied about not knowing Anne Meredith
 45 Chills
 46 Poltroon
 48 Bowling apparatus

51 Those who regret
52 Diphthong
*53 Ariadne's addiction
54 African region
55 Portmanteau
56 Babylonian storm god

57 Capture
58 Bridge joy
61 Ghost noise
63 Two: comb. form
68 Mary's title: abbrev.

1	2	3	4	5		6	7	8	9		10	11	12	13
14						15					16			
17			18			19				20				
21		22		23	24				25					
26			27				28							
			29			30					31	32		
33	34	35				36					37		38	
39					40					41				
42			43	44			45	46						
	47	48					49							
	50				51				52	53	54			
55	56	57			58				59					
60				61			62	63		64				
65			66			67		68						
69			70			71								

15

Death on the Nile

ACROSS

1 Psychedelic drug: abbrev.
4 Villain Vader
* 8 _____ House, honeymoon site
12 Holy Solar Disc: Egyptian
14 Chess term: abbrev.
15 Beloved of Zeus
16 Arab letter
*17 He went from estate manager to millionaire: 2 wds.
20 Place confidence in
*21 Next to gain as prime motive according to Poirot
*22 Wadi Halfa excursion was made by _____
23 Suffix forming diminutive
*24 _____ Hall, Linnet Ridgeway's home
*26 Mr. Ferguson's opinion of Dr. Bessner
*29 Poirot's winter vacation spot, chosen for climate
31 Greater London Council: abbrev.
*34 What Jackie de Bellefort could be at times
35 Rumanian silver coin
37 Dawn goddess
38 Vous _____ , you are: French
39 Clocks or cheese, e.g.
41 Anthony's lady
43 On: Scottish
44 Intra-uterine device: abbrev.
*45 Dr. Bessner's lenses
46 Controversial aircraft: abbrev.
47 Mexican sun-worshipping tribe
49 Exclamations of disgust
*50 Salome Otterbourne's novel, Under the Fig _____
51 Woman of quality
*54 Poirot to Jackie — "Do not open your _____ to evil"
*57 She was ashamed of her mother
60 Keenness
*61 Adjunct to Poirot's meal of quality: 2 wds.
*64 _____ Hartz, Linnet's mother
65 Hospital device: abbrev.
66 Biblical name
67 Mob scene
68 Raised platform
69 Adage
70 One: Scottish

DOWN

1 Spanish article
2 Incite
3 Commune
4 Did not: abbrev.
5 Orbital point farthest from Earth
6 Until: abbrev.
7 Garden tool
8 She was in love with would-be bigamist
9 Elevation: abbrev.
10 It was toured up to Luxor
11 On fire: comp. wd., arch.
13 Salome's profession
18 Snare
19 The: arch.
22 Radio Direction Tuner: abbrev.
24 Yods
25 Work: Latin
*26 Miss Bowers felt they were camel adjuncts
27 Conspiring imposter, Titus _____
28 Denotes origin: suffix
30 Slip easily
*32 She was accompanied by 62 Down to police station
*33 Tour of 10 Down
*36 Her shawl muffled shot
39 Comparative measurement
40 Wit: arch.
42 Bind: comb. form
47 Singer Garfunkel
48 Small compartment
50 Treasurer: abbrev.
52 Star: prefix

53 Mother
54 Top
55 Woman's name
56 Fire god: Hindu
57 Sun god: Egyptian

58 Hip bones
59 Black
*61 He also had mother trouble
62 Egg: prefix
63 Devoured

Cat Among the Pigeons

ACROSS

* 1 Scotland Yard department that Adam Goodman wasn't in: abbrev.
4 Early Irish alphabet
8 Church office
*12 Ronnie's pseudonym
14 Sum up
*16 Miss Rich went on about him at length
17 Brain tissue
*18 She was in the gym
19 Scottish alders
20 Tune
21 Exist
*22 He ran "Your Garden" column in *Sunday Mail*
*24 Jennifer Sutcliffe's godmother, Aunt _____
26 As written: music
*27 She was thin, dark, intense and a psychology graduate
30 Than: Scottish
32 Id est: abbrev.
33 Noun forming diminutive: suffix
36 Miscarry
37 Field
39 South African region
40 Pure
41 Elegant apartment
43 Otherwise
44 Assistant: abbrev.
45 Babylonian god
*46 Sergeant who took call on games mistress's murder
47 Golf apparatus
48 Early Dutch geographer
49 Pronoun
51 Hooded snake
52 Arab name
53 Islam priest: var.
55 Strolls
58 Note
59 Gremlin, e.g.
62 Japanese court
63 Roman river
66 Dear: Italian
68 Ericsson
*69 Ruth _____ , the United States tennis pro Princess Shaista wished to emulate
70 Reckon
71 Alaskan city
72 Street
73 Title: Hindu

DOWN

* 1 Eileen Rich felt one amongst them
2 Notion
3 Artist Salvadore
4 Church instrument
* 5 Taught by Eleanor Vansittart
6 Fiddler crab genus
7 Man's nickname
8 Huntress
9 Exchange for labor
10 Fire god: Hindu
11 Snoot
*13 Bully's secretary
*15 Gulf that Jennifer was taken to
23 Origin-denoting suffix
25 International: abbrev.
*27 Ali Yusuf's country
28 Overweight
29 More reprehensible
31 Moslem name of God
33 Man's name
34 Powerful light beam
35 Constantine's saintly mom
*39 Lady Carlton Sanways, closet sot
*41 She wanted bosoms
42 Irish poet's pseudonym
46 Ground-Controlled Approach: abbrev.
48 Strong beer
*50 Psychic English mistress
*52 She chose an emerald
54 WWI battle site

DOWN continued

*55 Mrs. Sutcliffe and her daughter
were flown there
56 Japanese ship
57 Cup rim
60 Buddhist spirit of evil

61 Booty: obs.
64 Sick
65 Bachelor of Liberal Arts: abbrev.
67 Unsorted flour: Indian

The Body in the Library

ACROSS

1 Mine: Cornish
* 4 Raymond Starr once sold them
9 Recede
*12 Hugo McLean felt Raymond looked like one
*13 Ruby Keene's real surname
*14 Pamela Reeves' home, Daneleigh ____
15 Son of Sif
16 Entertainers' society: abbrev.
17 Babylonian mother goddess
*18 A blond body was found thereupon
*20 Her bad ankle gave Ruby a chance
22 Canal-passage in the brain
23 Closely confined
24 Fused: comb. form
*26 Basil Blake's cottage was "closed in a hideous shell of half timbering and ____ ____ ": 2 wds.
*31 She bit her nails
33 White: comb. form
34 Mountain: prefix
35 Axillary
36 Cotton thread
38 ____ Well that Ends Well
39 Biblical name
40 Sun god: Egyptian
*41 Mrs. Price ____ , she carried news to the vicar
*43 Ruby was missing from this town
46 Lines indicating mystic power sources in United Kingdom
47 Carter and Yutang, e.g.
48 Payment for Charon
50 Cut
*53 Conway Jefferson's dead wife
57 Wing-like part
58 Chamber pot
60 Iodine: French
61 Extremities
62 Third stomach of cow: plural
63 Rangoon distance measure
64 Protecting shelter
65 Arab republic
66 Before: arch.

DOWN

1 Great evil: arch.
2 Hebrew acrostic
* 3 Bantry butler
* 4 He dressed outrageously
5 Belonging to chief Norse gods
6 The Great Canadian Novel: abbrev.
7 Personal guides assigned at birth by God: abbrev.
* 8 Murder month
9 Receive for work
*10 ____ Boar, pub
14 Taste for objets d'art
17 Great ____ , constellation
19 Short Take Off and Landing: abbrev.
21 To
23 Satiate
24 Helmet-like part
25 With all one's might: arch.
27 Has not: abbrev.
*28 She called Miss Marple immediately
29 Subordinary bearings: heraldic
*30 ____ Legge
31 Spotted cat
32 Candy bar: 2 wds.
37 Notes of debt: abbrev.
*39 Her husband's unwise speculations left her financial position precarious
40 Friend: French
42 Tagalog river
44 Fairy types
45 Harsh and grating
49 William Jennings ____
50 Phone
51 Opposed to aweather

DOWN continued

52 Ire
53 Mr. America: 2 wds., abbrev.
54 Lion's yell
*55 Mrs. Chetty's youngest
*56 _____ Little Indians
59 Friend or neighbor

What Mrs. McGillicuddy Saw! (4:50 from Paddington)

ACROSS

1 Russian country house
6 New Testament book
10 Picnic crashers
*14 She confirmed Harold Crackenthorpe's alibi for December 20th
*15 Alfred Crackenthorpe's not quite legal gang, "The _____ lot"
16 Fishing gear
*17 Bryan Eastley's dead wife
18 Usually valid
19 Scarlett's home
20 Knock
21 Between D and F Wings: 2 wds.
*23 Lucy Eyelesbarrow's mark in mathematics at Oxford
24 23rd Greek letter
25 Maidens
26 Biblical twin whose body was "like a hairy mantle"
*29 She did the Crackenthorpe brasses three days a week: 2 wds.
31 Central leaf vein
33 Hurt
34 American Journal of Archaeology: abbrev.

*37 _____ Road, address of faithful Florence
*39 Rutherford Hall gardener
41 Chalice
42 Seed covering
44 Classifying
*45 He showed Alexander and James the body in barn
46 Mirth
47 The cock crowed _____ at betrayal
50 Long-tailed Indian ape
52 Spanish monetary units
53 Blood vessel: comb. form
55 Eastern title
58 Brazil tree
*59 Mrs. McGillicuddy bought her a rabbit
*60 Local inspector initially in charge of case
62 Draw over surface
63 Irish exclamation
*64 Father of Alexander
66 Water: comb. form
67 Big Four conference point

DOWN

1 Stag
2 Actor Alan
3 Haircut
4 Success
5 Man's Biblical end
6 Italian wine
* 7 He was consulted by Miss Marple and Mrs. McGillicuddy
8 Cult assassin
9 Wooden tub: dialect
*10 Cedric Crakenthorpe's profession
11 Comes close
12 Succinct
13 Staves

*22 He came down specially from London at great inconvenience to attend inquest
23 Steadily
24 Yellow; Indian
*25 Madame Joliet's ballet company
*26 Beloved of Dr. Quimper
27 Asian country
28 Po tributary
30 Exclamation
32 Hayes and Newton, e.g.
34 East Indian vine
*35 Her fish bone revealed murderer
36 Angel: French

DOWN continued

38 Animal nest
40 Ladies' Professional Golfers' Association: abbrev.
*43 "Maps of all kinds were his passion"
45 Fodder into feed
47 Commerce
*48 Ex-Scotland Yard commissioner
49 Tracking device: abbrev.

*51 Mrs. McGillicuddy bought him a space gun
53 Eagles' home
54 Growl: obs.
55 Acid radical
56 Zeus's foster mother
*57 She was a devout Catholic
59 Jehovah
61 Altar constellation

<table>
<tr><td>1</td><td>2</td><td>3</td><td>4</td><td>5</td><td>■</td><td>6</td><td>7</td><td>8</td><td>9</td><td>■</td><td>10</td><td>11</td><td>12</td><td>13</td></tr>
<tr><td>14</td><td></td><td></td><td></td><td></td><td>■</td><td>15</td><td></td><td></td><td></td><td>■</td><td>16</td><td></td><td></td><td></td></tr>
<tr><td>17</td><td></td><td></td><td></td><td></td><td>■</td><td>18</td><td></td><td></td><td></td><td>■</td><td>19</td><td></td><td></td><td></td></tr>
<tr><td>20</td><td></td><td></td><td>■</td><td>21</td><td>22</td><td></td><td></td><td>■</td><td>23</td><td></td><td></td><td></td><td></td><td></td></tr>
<tr><td>■</td><td>■</td><td>24</td><td></td><td></td><td>■</td><td></td><td>■</td><td>25</td><td></td><td></td><td></td><td></td><td></td><td></td></tr>
<tr><td>26</td><td>27</td><td>28</td><td></td><td>■</td><td>29</td><td></td><td>30</td><td></td><td></td><td></td><td>■</td><td>■</td><td>■</td><td>■</td></tr>
<tr><td>31</td><td></td><td></td><td>32</td><td></td><td>■</td><td>33</td><td></td><td></td><td>■</td><td>34</td><td>35</td><td>36</td><td></td><td></td></tr>
<tr><td>37</td><td></td><td></td><td></td><td>38</td><td>■</td><td>39</td><td></td><td>40</td><td></td><td></td><td></td><td></td><td></td><td></td></tr>
<tr><td>41</td><td></td><td></td><td>■</td><td>42</td><td>43</td><td>■</td><td>44</td><td></td><td></td><td></td><td></td><td></td><td></td><td></td></tr>
<tr><td>■</td><td>■</td><td>45</td><td></td><td></td><td></td><td></td><td>■</td><td>46</td><td></td><td></td><td></td><td></td><td></td><td></td></tr>
<tr><td>47</td><td>48</td><td>49</td><td></td><td></td><td>■</td><td>50</td><td>51</td><td></td><td>■</td><td>■</td><td>■</td><td></td><td></td><td></td></tr>
<tr><td>52</td><td></td><td></td><td>■</td><td>53</td><td>54</td><td></td><td></td><td>■</td><td>55</td><td>56</td><td>57</td><td></td><td></td><td></td></tr>
<tr><td>58</td><td></td><td></td><td>■</td><td>59</td><td></td><td></td><td>■</td><td>60</td><td>61</td><td></td><td></td><td></td><td></td><td></td></tr>
<tr><td>62</td><td></td><td></td><td>■</td><td>63</td><td></td><td></td><td>■</td><td>64</td><td></td><td></td><td></td><td></td><td></td><td></td></tr>
<tr><td>65</td><td></td><td></td><td>■</td><td>66</td><td></td><td></td><td>■</td><td>67</td><td></td><td></td><td></td><td></td><td></td><td></td></tr>
</table>

Nemesis

ACROSS

* 1 "One of the most frightening words there is in the world"
5 Cleopatra's suicide weapons
9 Grapevine disease
13 Poison arrow
14 Plug
*15 _____ , Hants, Walters' new home
16 Town
17 Caste
*18 This and red were the colors of assailant's pullover
19 Water street in Venice
*20 Who Miss Marple met on St. Honore
21 Woman's name
22 Godfrey and Conan Doyle, e.g.
24 Cattle genus
25 Over there: arch.
26 Gate
28 Citizens' Band Information: abbrev.
31 Jerk: Hebrew slang
*33 "Sly, sexy little village girl": 2 wds.

35 Loyal
36 Cap, e.g.
37 Upon the top of
*38 Walters' married name: 2 wds.
40 Belonging to a duke
41 Explosive: abbrev.
42 Heavy rainfall
43 Ballet apparel
44 Senora: abbrev.
*45 How Miss Marple described herself to Mr. Rafiel
48 Right: comb. form
51 Root forms of words
53 Luna's mate
54 Relating to the Trojan War
55 Oceanic tunicate
56 Christina's nickname
*57 Miss Bartlett's other name
58 Utensil
*59 Miss Marple's niece-in-law
60 Nine: comb. form
61 Domestic slave
62 Institution: abbrev.

DOWN

1 The Scales
2 Dream: comb. form
* 3 Thought to be 33 Across: 2 wds.
4 Electroencephalogram: abbrev.
5 Teutonic Olympus
6 Facing glacier
* 7 Assailant's sweater type
8 Biblical measure
9 Greece
10 Headline
11 South American narcotic shrub
12 Symbol of eternal life: Egyptian
15 Assimilate
20 Jupiter's wife
23 Zeroed
*24 Golden _____ , hotel on tour
26 Sorrow
27 Prayer

*28 43 Down's death wound
29 Philippine servant
30 Symbol of deity
31 Proofreader's OK
32 Common swift
33 Caucasian race in China
34 Line of travel
36 Malay boat
*39 He and Joanna Crawford witnessed attack: 2 wds.
40 Russian council
*43 She was told that Miss Marple had come on pilgrimage
44 Vampire's end
45 Synthetic fabric
46 Belonging to Inner Hebrides Island
47 Angular plane

24

*48 Cherry called this and kidneys
     "Chinese Dinner"
49 North Carolina college
50 Descendant

51 Town near Padua
52 Town in New Mexico
56 Dutch East Indian weight

1	2	3	4		5	6	7	8			9	10	11	12
13					14					15				
16					17					18				
19					20					21				
22			23						24					
		25					26	27				28	29	30
31	32					33					34			
35					36						37			
38				39						40				
41					42					43				
			44					45					46	47
48	49	50				51	52					53		
54						55					56			
57						58					59			
60						61					62			

Sleeping Murder

ACROSS

* 1 Fortunately Mrs. Hengrave's kitchen already had one
* 4 Ginger _____ , where Miss Marple met Giles and Gwenda Reed
 7 Foul-tempered giant
 11 Any araceous plant
 13 Afresh
*15 "Mine _____ dazzle"
*16 He treated Major Halliday
 18 Plant exudate
 20 Thing: Latin
*21 She made great gingerbread
*22 Formerly St. Catherine's
 24 Deity of darkness: Egyptian
*26 Consumed at 4 Across
 27 Spanish river
*30 Color of 22 Across
 33 Jot
*37 Interviewed by Gwenda, she still lived in Dillmouth
 39 Stubborn
 41 Educable mentally retarded: abbrev.
*42 Its insides were painted mustard-cum-biscuit

 43 Midnight: abbrev.
*44 Alison _____ , Gwenda's aunt
 46 Chemical suffix
 47 Tail
*49 Miss Marple found Easton's _____ helpful
*50 Inspector with Longford police
 52 United States Army Information Dept: abbrev.
 54 Assent
 55 Vedic cloud dragon
 57 Imbibe
*59 Royal _____ Hotel in Dillmouth
*63 Major with maniacally jealous wife
 68 Sound collector
 69 Alkali
*70 Doctor and Saltmarsh superintendent
 71 One: German
*73 "She _____ young"
 75 Third largest Philippine Is.
 76 Russian liquid measure
 77 Quiet!
 78 Nor: arch.

DOWN

 1 Specified place
* 2 Prized possession of Giles's aunt
 3 English river
 4 Replaced by K in Old English
 5 Indefinite article
 6 Low caste Hindu
 7 Old English: abbrev.
 8 Brain ridges
* 9 He bought Hillside
 10 Actual being: Latin
 11 Apparatus: abbrev.
 12 Specks
*14 "Mr. Sobersides"
 17 Ragout
 19 Noun forming diminutive: suffix
 23 Hand or hack, e.g.

*25 A proper mouser and hater of ribbons
 27 Missouri town
*28 Orphan who travelled a lot
 29 Atlantic: abbrev.
*31 Gwenda's birthplace
*32 The slashing of this net to ribbons puzzled gardener
*34 Mrs. Fane's asthmatic spaniel
 35 Infuse
 36 Parasite in blood: abbrev.
 37 Love of darkness
 38 Item doffed
 40 Yards: abbrev.
 45 Hindu title
 48 Fallen

51 Pitch
53 Flat circular form
*56 "Cover _____ face"
58 Dowels
59 Third letters
60 Milk: French
61 Cartoonist
62 Chinese distance measure

64 Malayan title of respect
65 Alas!
66 Monitor lizard
67 Uncle to Saul
*70 Gwenda's mother's initials
72 Eastern front: abbrev.
74 It: German

The Secret Adversary

ACROSS

1 Exclamation of dismay
* 5 Jane Finn's father, oil-steel-rail magnate
9 Fried: French
13 Change for five
14 Witch-hunter territory
16 Charged
17 Until: arch.
18 Mary _____ Moore
19 And others: Latin, abbrev., 2 wds.
20 Saul's uncle
21 Old World plant of lily family
22 Yellow fruit
*24 Kramenin's secretary
26 _____ and the Man
27 Light time
*28 Signature on note
*32 Most celebrated KC in England
35 Stomachs
36 Beget
37 Son of Judah
38 Dutch village
39 Broad bean
40 Army, e.g.
41 Brown shade
*42 Julius Hersheimmer's father
*43 Doctor treating Jane
*45 Albert's name for Tuppence's job
46 Tetragrammaton
*47 Mrs. Vandemeyer died of an overdose of this
51 Master: French
54 Klip's mate
55 Numeral
56 Eject
57 Cold
*59 Mr. Brown was member of fabled 2 Down _____
60 Russian sea
61 Based on Mohammed's life and words
62 Other: Latin
63 Allowance
64 Tereus's son
65 Ass: German

DOWN

* 1 _____ Adventurers Ltd.
* 2 Mr. Brown was member of fabled _____ 59 Across
3 Rock: comb. form
4 Within: comb. form
* 5 _____ Priors
6 Elected official
7 To pour scorn on: arch.
8 Look
9 To strip of blubber or skin
*10 "Ready _____ they call her in the States"
*11 First name of 24 Across
12 Brain tissue
*15 He was rumored to be the "master criminal of this age": 2 wds.
21 Down with: French, 2 wds.
23 Current measures
25 Primal garden
26 Cognizant
28 Figure of speech
29 Close
30 Pepper shrub
31 Charitable gift: Hindu
32 Indian millet
33 Year: Latin
34 Indian native servant
35 Sofa
*38 He gave oilskin to Jane
39 Trifle: arch.
41 Wild goat
42 Aid
*44 _____ Willie, Julius's "friend"
*45 Lieutenant _____ Beresford
47 French city
48 Disturbs
*49 Tuppence took her place
50 With authority of law
*51 _____ House, Ebury, Yorkshire

52 Astral form
53 Danube tributary
54 English county
58 Hawaiian assembly
59 Sailyard: Scottish

1	2	3	4		5	6	7	8			9	10	11	12
13					14				15		16			
17					18						19			
20				21					22	23				
24			25				26							
			27			28					29	30	31
32	33	34			35						36			
37				38						39				
40				41					42					
43			44				45							
			46				47			48	49	50		
51	52	53				54					55			
56				57	58				59					
60				61					62					
63				64				65						

N or M?

ACROSS

1 Second months: abbrev.
5 First man
* 9 The "song" of the agent's message
13 Idea: comb. form
14 Withered
16 Arrow poison
17 _____ and starts
18 Canonical hour
19 Yarn
20 Explosive: abbrev.
21 Placed on a peg
*22 Dentist who lent out his office
*24 Local ARP warden whose butler was suspicious
26 Woman's name
27 Harvester, e.g.
*28 Discovered by Tommy in bathroom
*32 Mr. Meadowes
35 First Jewish ecclesiastical month
*36 Carrot _____ , Derek's nickname for Tommy
37 Wing-like part

38 Turpentine yielding tree
*39 She held Tuppence at gunpoint
40 _____ culpa
41 Scottish accents
42 Boasts
*43 _____ Blenkensop
45 Wheeled vehicle
46 Olympian troublemaker who threw golden apple
*47 Mr. Grant's signal
51 Support
54 Makes mistake
55 Antiquity
56 With: French
57 Senior
59 Sicilian resort
60 Civil wrong
61 Musical composition type
62 Frosts
63 High and low, e.g.
64 Narcotic shrub
*65 "Smuggler's _____ ," home of 24 Across

DOWN

* 1 "M" was one head of this Column
2 Missouri town
* 3 She was twice-adopted
* 4 Snored message
5 Between planets
* 6 Flyer son of Tuppence and Tommy
7 Dry
8 Thirteenth letter in Hebrew alphabet
9 Sign
10 Philippines Is. termite
11 Rex Stout's beer-drinking detective
12 Swiss herdsman
*15 Her job was very hush-hush
*21 Treacherous cohort of 15 Down
23 Peace: comb. form

25 Agatha Christie's title
26 Musical records
28 Irish lament
29 Spirit lamp
*30 Agent's message sounded like " _____ Susie"
31 Resorts
32 Drive in
33 Olive genus
34 Egyptian goddess of truth
35 Nose opening
*38 Mr. Grant felt that his quest for personal glory was akin to the traitors'
39 Irish exclamation
41 Spin
42 Lounges
44 Responds
*45 _____ Top

*47 Nurse _____ Elton
48 Jig, e.g.
49 Woman's name
50 Leavening
*51 The Duck and Dog publican

52 Maenad's cry
53 Zeus' wife
58 Baldur's slayer
59 Goddess of healing

By the Pricking of My Thumbs

ACROSS

* 1 _____ Wing
  5 Chills
  10 Crutch
*14 Water _____ , ancient name of Perry house
  15 Mushrooms
  16 Stop
  17 Babylonian war god
*18 Sunny _____ , Ada's retirement home
  19 Dolphin genus
  20 Parson bird
*21 _____ Waters, name on gravestone
*22 Villagers called her Nellie
*23 Amos' wife
  25 Jai _____ , Spanish game
  27 Beware of Dog: Latin, abbrev.
  29 Egg
*30 Emma Boscowan's work
*34 It had many names
  36 Enterprising Vulcan
  37 Before: arch.
  38 Teen complaint

*39 Amos _____
  40 Commanded
  41 Medical Officer in Charge: abbrev.
  42 Killed
  43 Scheduled
*44 It was originally Mrs. Lancaster's
  46 Elevator cage
  47 The Three _____
  48 Organs of sight
*49 "Cocoa lady"
  51 Cleansing agent
  54 Reaps' mate
  55 Weep: Scottish
  58 Hebrew measure
*59 34 Across was situated here
  61 Three: German
  62 Inland Russian sea
  63 Join
  64 Related
  65 Neat
  66 Girl's name
*67 Albert discovered its secret compartment

DOWN

  1 Send
  2 Holy Buddhist mount
* 3 Fanshaw's middle name
* 4 Fanshaw's first name
* 5 Reported location of Mrs. Johnson
  6 Cunning
  7 Wavy: Heraldry
  8 Incite, _____ on
  9 Sift: Scottish
*10 Sir _____ Starke
  11 Hindu queen
  12 Few: comb. form
  13 World-maker: Egyptian
  21 Animated
  22 Stop short
  24 Fail to maintain
  25 Oak seed
  26 Girl's name

  27 Bite noisily
*28 Morphine vehicle
*30 Bridge House realtor
  31 Set of workers
  32 Dictate
  33 River grasses
  35 Claw: zoology
  36 O'Casey and Connery, e.g.
  39 Closed, as wings
*40 It opened the "priest's hole"
  42 Charon's route
  43 New Mexican town
  45 Almost
*46 Name Tuppence signed into hospital with
  49 Watery enclosures
*50 Mrs. Lancaster's name at Rosetrellis
*51 Added to Emma's piece

52 Biblical king
53 Foretell, as with cards
54 State of agitation
56 Plural of real
*57 Waterside's color

59 Bowl
60 Collection of notes on particular subject
61 Mom's mate

Postern of Fate

ACROSS

1 Nickname of actress/singer Streisand
5 Woman's name
*10 Alleged patriot
14 Askew: Scottish
15 Uric acid salt
*16 On Tuppence's list
*17 Tommy's nickname: 2 wds.
*19 She claimed to be gardener
20 Eager
21 Guy-rope
22 Glide
23 Biblical judge
24 Indian hemp shrub
*26 She was with children's hospital
*29 Counted by Mr. Robinson
33 Scientific study: abbrev.
*34 Name that Mary Jordan was always known by
35 Cadmus's daughter
36 Back of neck
37 Full of froth
38 Jason's ship
39 Brazilian wallaba tree
40 Trunks
*41 Pensioners' 44 Down _____
*42 "Mary Jordan did not die naturally. _____ of us": 3 wds.
44 She told Scarlett O'Hara she knew all about birthing babies
46 Greek goddess of victory
47 Settled
48 Tibetan raccoon cousin
51 Found in Gilead
52 Man's name
55 Sandarac tree
*56 The Beresfords' new address: 2 wds.
*59 Broken by 19 Across as distraction
*60 Henry's gardening grandfather
61 Rebecca's elder twin son
62 Enough: arch.
63 _____ Blind Mice
64 Machine gun

DOWN

1 Wrote Brandenburg Concertos
2 Hamitic language
* 3 Tall boy with squint, Junior Brigade member
4 Persian weight
* 5 _____ Chop, Tommy's friend
6 Indo-European
* 7 He went from publican to butler
8 WWII area: abbrev.
9 Lunar Excursion Module: abbrev.
*10 KK
11 _____ cadabra
12 Egyptian goddess of weaving and archery
13 Otherwise
18 Norwegian city
22 Sunny: Scottish
23 Substitution: suffix
24 Palma: comb. form
25 Solely
26 Central Hawaiian island
27 Unsuitable
28 Fruit of custard-apple relative
*29 Mathilde
30 Plies with drink: Scottish
*31 He was sent by Mr. Solomon
32 Clumsy fellow
34 French river
*37 Found in hole of bottom shelf
38 Corrosive
40 Rolled tea
*43 He hoped to be a poet
*44 Pensioners' _____ 41 Across
45 Red pine
47 Ancient: comb. form
48 Cover with stone
49 Islands near Galway
50 Nasal: comb. form
51 Ursine beast
*52 Swallow's _____ , old name of Beresford home
53 Wing-like part

54 Chinese measure of length
56 Return blow
57 Quiet!
58 Thing: Latin

1	2	3	4		5	6	7	8	9		10	11	12	13
14					15						16			
17				18							19			
20				21					22				
			23				24	25					
26	27	28					29					30	31	32
33					34						35		
36				37					38			
39			40					41			
42		43				44	45			
	46				47				
48	49	50				51				52	53	54
55				56				57			
58				59				60			
61				62				63			

The Pale Horse

ACROSS

1 Having heat
* 5 Architectural subject of Mark Easterbrook's book
*10 Pale Horse owner
14 Lamb's pen name
15 Spur of mountain
16 Character of Norse magical alphabet
17 Prizefighter
18 Cauls: var.
19 Philippine lizard
*20 Mrs. Davis's address
*22 Baron _____ , great 50 Down power
24 Negative and positive ones are in the air
25 Tramp
26 Hit on head: slang
*29 Police surgeon who found list on priest's body
33 German spa
*34 She was formerly of CRC
36 Got up
37 Grouse congregations
39 Narrow passages
41 Celtic
42 Candidate lists
44 Bovine mamma
46 Turf clump
*47 David _____ , History lecturer and Poppy's date
49 Poe's birds
51 Wheat fungus
52 Exchange premium
53 Visitor
*56 5 Down promised to protect her: 2 wds.
60 Hawaiian royal chief
61 Ave _____
*63 _____ Park, Mark's hotel
64 Character in Henry VI
65 Adjust
66 Kingly symbols
*67 Friend of Lou Ellis's
68 Witch time
69 Voodoo magic

DOWN

* 1 Halfwit, witch and housekeeper
2 Wing-like
3 Nothing: French
* 4 _____ Digby, name on list
* 5 Sybil's spirit control
6 Higher exams
7 Tingle with cold: Scottish
8 Shoshonean
9 One who leases
*10 Sadducismus Triumphatus, workbook
11 Hick
12 Arthurian lady
13 Bigfoot
21 Chopped earth
23 _____ cadabra
25 Sprayed
*26 Mark thought she sacrificied white cocks
27 Persian leader
28 Inquired
29 Girl's name
30 Juniper
*31 Beaded gourd holding snake bones
32 Wants
35 Safe
*38 Poppy's surname
*40 Detective _____ Lee
43 River channel
45 Sudden attack
*48 Mrs. Davis's confessor
*50 Ju-ju
52 On high: comp. word
53 Fortress commander
54 Actor Ray
55 Stead
56 Smartly dressed
57 Yugoslav native
58 Fat: comb. form

59 Latin she-bear
62 Mohammed's adopted son

1	2	3	4		5	6	7	8	9		10	11	12	13
14					15						16			
17					18						19			
20				21					22	23				
			24					25						
26	27	28					29					30	31	32
33				34		35				36				
37			38		39				40		41			
42				43		44				45		46		
47					48				49		50			
			51					52						
53	54	55					56					57	58	59
60					61	62					63			
64					65						66			
67					68						69			

37

Hallowe'en Party

ACROSS

1 Wide upholstered seat
5 Makes mistakes
9 Egyptian month
13 Leave out
14 Fear
16 Half: comb. form
*17 She shared flat with Nora Ambrose: 2 wds.
19 Blood carrier
*20 "Tall and superior"
21 Hurries
*22 Elspeth McKay's brother
24 Girl's name
25 Scandinavian giant
*26 Michael Garfield's ex-mistress
*29 Local witch
33 Plant louse
34 Large: comb. form
35 High: Chinese
36 Canal between North and Baltic Seas
37 Reinforced with fabric
38 Maori weapon
39 Enlisted: abbrev.
40 Recharge
41 Jibes: arch.
*42 Missing "opera" girl
*44 Judith Butler's mother-in-law
45 Kitty's rests
46 Lime tree
47 Tongue: comb. form
50 Pear
51 Within: comb. form
54 Baking chamber
*55 Fullerton, Harrison and _____
58 Mineral tar
59 Port on Davao Gulf
60 Shrub genus
61 Growl
62 Sci Fi writers, Lester and Judy-Lynn, the Del _____
*63 "Pussy's in the _____ ", Mrs. Goodbody's prophecy

DOWN

1 Soya
2 Sultanate
* 3 Ariadne Oliver's detective's nationality
4 Devoured
5 Girl's name
6 Flow: comb. form
7 Moslem chief
8 Occupied
9 Speech part
10 Opposes hammer face
11 Pertaining to Amide
*12 _____ Crest, home of 22 Across
*15 Nicky Ransome's buddy
18 Dilutes
23 Foot: comb. form
24 Linden tree
25 Yoga expert
26 Scrapes
27 Pronounce
28 Overcome
29 Thief: Hebrew
30 Giraffe cousin
*31 Apple substitutes
32 You: slang
34 Quarrels
*37 Joyce Reynold's brother, more obnoxious than she
38 Formerly Saul
40 DNAs mate
*41 She was slain by her own big mouth
43 To set with stars
44 Sappho's home
46 Present
*47 Poirot's research man
48 Girl's name
49 Dare: French
50 Silk in cocoon
51 Imitation: suffix
52 Blind, as hawks
53 Evangelist Roberts

56 It's given in listening
57 Tuesday's deity

Elephants Can Remember

ACROSS

1 Belonging to the American Medical Associatin: abbrev.
5 Abraham's wife
9 Filthy lucre
13 Foul
14 Muse of lyric poetry
16 Whistling swan
17 Occipital protuberances
*18 Button king
19 *Last Days of Pompeii* character
20 Droop
21 Greek letter
22 Mended
*24 Author of *The Second Goldfish*
26 Rockefeller concern
27 Oak genus
*28 His wife attended school with 24 Across
*32 Hatters _____ , Sussex, early Preston-Grey home
*35 Maurine _____ , attended writer luncheon
36 Professional Golfers' Association: abbrev.
37 Los Angeles team
38 Mimics
39 Darkens
*40 Poirot friend
41 Old: comb. form
*42 She gave wardrobe advice
*43 Wig-wearing twin
45 Cornish mine
46 Nothings
*47 Rumored cause of Ravenscroft deaths
51 Hitherto
54 Former Western Pakistani province
55 African worm
56 Minerals
*57 One of Ariadne Oliver's elephants
59 Ancient Briton
60 Atlanta sports arena
61 Novelist Jong
62 Pole: Spanish
63 A dog is _____ best friend
64 Not shut
65 Pool: Scottish

DOWN

* 1 City of saint who inspired Molly
* 2 Little Saltern _____ , Nanny's home
3 Excuse of being elsewhere
4 Small ocean
* 5 The _____ *Goldfish*, Oliver's work
6 Sharp-crested ridge in rugged mountains
7 Biblical word of reproach
8 New Zealand aborigine
* 9 He was brought into case by 24 Across
10 Esau's father-in-law
11 Isolated
*12 _____ Wizell, Ravenscroft gardener
*15 "_____ _____ have long shadows": 2 wds.
21 *Henry VI* character
23 Assistant: abbrev.
25 Mars
26 Olive oil: comb. form
28 Hermit: arch.
29 Armadillo
30 Kindle: comb. form
31 Essence: Hindu
32 Measure of weight
33 Hindu deity
34 Arab chief
35 Man's name
*38 Mrs. Buckle's daughter, sold cosmetics
39 Toilet powder

40

41 Couple
*42 Occupation of 42 Across
44 Secret knowledge
45 Babe's companion
47 Throughout
48 Regarding last division of small intestine
*49 "Poor, unhappy, hating"

*50 _____ Terrace, Ariadne's home
51 Explosive noise
52 Humorist Bombeck
*53 Natural mother of Desmond Burton-Cox
54 Clip to bits
58 Nigerian Negro
59 Corporal: abbrev.

The Secret of Chimneys

ACROSS

1 East European
5 To confuse
10 Actress West
13 Indian healers of southwestern United States
14 Small egg
15 Promise's mate
16 Maple genus
17 What summer television stations did
18 Slave: Anglo-Saxon
*19 Mr. Holme's firm: Balderson and ____
21 Removes
23 This month: arch.
24 Eject
25 Divorce city
*27 Boris claimed he directed pistol: 2 wds.
31 Charmed: French
33 That which is used
34 Ail: arch.
35 Thought form
36 Modernist painter
37 Healing goddess
38 Monks
40 Minced oath
*41 She and Bill were in constant attendance to George Lomax: 2 wds.
44 Hindu goddess of beauty
45 Island in Visayan Islands, Philippines
46 Hooks
48 Belief in transcendent and immanent god(s)
*50 Queen Varaga's claimed ancestry
54 Precipitation
55 Omit
57 Hatred: Italian
58 Prompting
59 Stomach
60 Bacteriologist's wire
61 Anglo-Saxon letter
62 Discharge
63 Cheers

DOWN

1 Persian leader
2 Crazy: Spanish
3 Mimicked
* 4 Nee Cawthorn, Tim Revel's widow
* 5 ____ Anchoukoff, valet
6 Social occasions
7 Animal slaughter booty
8 Palm leaf
* 9 She was formerly with Countess de Breteuil
10 She was the "youngest and most skittish" of tour group: 2 wds.
11 Skin blemish
12 Supplements
15 Filter
20 Know: arch.
22 Eastern staple
24 Prussian spa
25 Forearm bones
*26 Lomax's dogs'-body
28 Oklahoma city
29 Helena: dim., var.
30 Dregs
31 Oxhide strap
*32 Penciled on M. Lemoine's cuff
*36 Count Stylptitch knew location of this
38 Movie, *The Seven Little* ____
39 High card
42 French river
*43 His grave was part of Anthony Cade's tour
44 Small: Scottish
47 Catkin
48 Real
49 Adamant
50 Frost

51 Theaters
*52 He was not really interested in
   first editions
53 Enemies
56 Carry laboriously

The Man in the Brown Suit

ACROSS

1 Sail yards: Scottish
* 5 _____ Grunberg, actress
10 Cape
14 Land measure
15 New Zealand native
16 Himalayan monkshood
*17 Obstinate Christian reverend
19 Dip
20 And others: Latin, abbrev.
21 Coptic bishop
*22 Anne Beddingfeld's shipboard nickname
*23 Harry Parker's telegram pseudonym
24 John: Irish
26 Noises
*29 Month on dropped paper?
32 Mountain lake
*33 Nationality of Dutchman's servants
34 South African underground stream
36 Migratory worker
37 Sited

38 African gazelle
39 Wordplay
40 Cathartic plants
41 Well: French
*42 Inspector _____ , "a small man with a ginger head"
44 Hastening
46 Royal Academy of Dramatic Arts, London: abbrev.
*47 Strike here had secret causes
*48 General who ought to receive documents
51 Element
52 Pull
*55 " _____ Ball Man," accident victim?
*56 Source of stench in Anne's cabin
59 Two-toed sloth
60 Warble
61 Blood-related
62 Himalayan wild goat
63 Exposed
64 Conifer

DOWN

* 1 He proposed to Anne
2 Eight: German
* 3 Colonel Race's pseudonym
4 Dry: French
5 Reparation
* 6 *Daily Budget* owner
7 Infinitesimal amount
8 Three: Spanish
9 Appearance
*10 Mill House body
11 On top of: comp. word
12 Drinks slowly
13 Discover
18 Help
22 Indian wild ox
*23 Monkey Man's daughter
24 Receptacles for valuables
25 Authoress Blyton
26 Desist

27 Seam caulker
28 Doctor's specimen
*29 Gardener whom Sir Eustace Pedler kept for wife's cooking
30 Lines from a circle's center to edge
31 Chinese government official residence
33 Fierce Plains Indian tribe
35 _____ Lardne
37 Estate not held by feudal tenure
38 In bed: comp. word
40 Ohio college town and town in Oklahoma
*43 _____ Minks, alias 17 Across
*44 John _____ Eardsley
45 Poison, arrow
47 Firearm
48 Lampblack

49 Da Vinci subject
50 Western state
51 Light
*52 Rhodesian threepence
53 Norse god, rune-owner

54 Lessen
56 Unsorted flour: Indian
57 Fortunate: Indian
58 Spigot

Crooked House

ACROSS

1 Soybean
5 To show: comb. form
10 Yell
14 Smell
15 Pertaining to hours
16 On the lee: comp. word
*17 She was terminally ill: 2 wds.
18 Lean
19 Alder tree: Scottish
20 What commanders did
21 Horizontal contour
22 Stated
24 Cheese type
26 Buses, e.g: abbrev.
*29 He was referred to as "Sweetie Pie"
33 Flags
34 Pledge: arch.
35 Woman's name
36 Lean animal: Scottish
37 Borough in Cheshire, United Kingdom
38 Welles movie, Citizen _____
39 Compass direction: abbrev.
40 Moan of pain
*41 Star of *Jezebel*
*42 They contained eserine
44 Rule
45 Contest
46 Caste
47 Rowdy: slang
49 Mr. Calloway
50 Attempt
53 Mahogany tree: Indian
*54 "Little crooked house": 2 wds.
*57 Nannie, Janet _____
58 Evangelist McPherson
59 United States Marine Corps: abbrev.
60 Lives precariously
61 Flies
62 Shrub genus

DOWN

* 1 Josephine Leonides' last promised treat
2 Baltic river
3 He painted 29 Across
4 Place of supplication: Latin
* 5 He was humiliated by the will
6 Placed in pits
7 City in western Rumania
8 Woman's name
9 Old times: arch.
*10 "Bally"
11 Other: Latin
*12 Stage name of 41 Across
13 Allow
*21 Ferdinand
22 Cut
23 Balaam's animal
*24 "A complete rabbit"
25 Prescribed manner
*26 Number of 44 Down
27 State of weather in spring
28 Author of *Tiny Alice*
29 Places
30 Reflection
31 Tree: comb. form
32 Mediterranean sea
34 Figure of speech
37 Arquebus support
38 Javanese language
*40 Doctor who x-rayed Josephine
41 Bon _____
43 Useless bees
*44 "Eleven _____ would have been more apposite" according to Charles Hayward
*46 She drank Josephine's cocoa
*47 Black _____ , Josephine's record
48 "Battle Hymn of the Republic" author
49 Peak: Italian
50 Trial
51 Branch

52 Peruvian Indian tribe
53 Three: Italian
54 Droop
55 Finish first
56 Duet

Endless Night

ACROSS

1 Stroke-shot in golf
* 5 Honeymoon spot
* 9 She was given cottage by Major Phillpot
*12 Gipsy _____
13 Love: Italian
15 Bee house
*16 Doctor with kindly manner
17 Uncultivated areas
18 Baker's tool
19 _____ Little Indians
20 Power: comb. form
*21 Old name of house
*23 Uncle Joe was killed here
25 Good humor
27 To be: Spanish
28 Colors
29 Freight bill: abbrev.
*31 Conquer
33 _____ Haute, city in western Indiana
34 Mountain: comb. form
35 Turkish regiment
36 _____ and outs
37 Solar disc: Egyptian

*38 Subject of Ellie's song
39 Trap
*41 He was a trustee and banker
42 Norse war god
*43 Queen _____ , Andrew Lippencott's vehicle across ocean
44 Caviar
*45 She "smelt and looked and tasted of sex"
47 Speech
49 Atmosphere
51 Russian fighter planes: abbrev.
52 Experimental place
55 Egyptian goddess of fertility
*56 Other half of Crawford's firm
*58 _____ Dog, cafe
59 Citizen _____ , movie
60 "Pomp and Circumstance" composer
*61 Name of cottage given to Mother Lee
62 Urge: Scottish
63 Ares
64 Seemly

DOWN

1 Egyptian lunar goddess
2 Pain
* 3 "He looks like a crook. . . .All that. . .bonhomie"
4 Not many
* 5 Lippincott's profession
6 Ammonia compound: comb. form
7 Russian weight
8 Fort
9 Organ
10 Always
11 Evens: arch.
*14 Old Mother Lee
15 Hollow: Scottish
20 Dread: Scottish
22 Bacteriologist's wire
24 Bone: comb. form

*25 This was laid on Ellie
*26 "Little white ridiculous temple-looking place"
*28 Uncle and car-crash victim
29 Scandinavian love goddess
*30 London street where Michael never considered buying shoes
31 Weapon handle
32 Light form
33 Crown
34 Ordo Templi Orientis: abbrev.
37 Actor Guinness
39 Widgeon
*40 Doctor known as "Leave-it-to- _____ -Shaw"
41 Woman's name
*44 Michael _____
45 Gleam brightly

46 Levitate
*47 He was "young and earnest"
*48 _____ Fenella
*49 He hired Rudolf Santonix
50 Munich's river

51 Great: prefix
53 Distance measure: French
54 Mangel-wurtzel, e.g.
57 Shade tree
58 Jesus' mother: abbrev.

The Mysterious Affair at Styles

ACROSS

* 3 The caterer in Tadminster
* 6 Poirot retrieved one from flower bed
* 9 How John and Lawrence referred to Emily
*10 Mr Raikes's occupation
*11 John lit it in Emily's bedroom
 12 This relative is mostly legal
 13 Cretan king tumbles into sleep
*14 Never cleared the coffee cups away
*16 Young William was one
*17 It was small, purple, with a Yale lock
 18 Urge ahead for yuletide drink (3, 3)
*22 Alfred bought strychnine to poison one

*24 Nailed in Antwerp
 25 Curtailed serf reveals Pole
 28 Saw reveals what sounds like Bea's past
*29 Lawyer and coroner
*30 What blood does
 33 This body is mostly hills
 34 Article looks inside teetotalers for tap
 35 Englishman and catholic stand in front of home to find dessert
*36 "Dark, ferret-faced man"
 37 This mountain climber carries a garbled message for help
*38 Worked regularly on the land

DOWN

* 1 Witnessed Emily's new will
* 2 The character of Emily's convulsions
 4 Arabian coast revealed in moan
* 5 Styles _____ _____ (2, 3)
* 6 8 was afraid of obliterating any of these
 7 This covering is mostly made of a young sheep and men
* 8 Had often stayed at Styles as a boy
 15 Depenultimize eager

*16 Emily died in one
 19 German, North American and Welshman nibble
*20 Evie's position
*21 _____ Arms
 23 Gasps alternately
*26 What Emily's sleeping powders were not
*27 Alfred wore them
*28 Purchased Emily's new will form
 31 These huts contain a woman
 32 Sounds like this level was a drop

The Murder of Roger Ackroyd

ACROSS

* 1 Died on a Thursday
* 4 How one died
* 7 Eliot's mill was on it
* 9 Saw Dr. Sheppard about her knee
  11 Behead a tyke
*13 Baby shoe belonged to him
  15 The barn roost concealed the leaders of the back-up navy
  17 I slam Ireland and Canada to favor Moslem culture
  19 Decapitate archly
*20 Discovered in summer house

  22 A Californian city functions after A, B — some articles!
  24 Broken shoe a prophet
  26 That wit Terry reveals his nervous state
  28 A portion for Abraham's nephew
*30 Elderly patient of Dr. Sheppard's
  32 Bog holds sticky mess
*33 Melrose was the chief one
  34 Young Edward gripped oar and rowed

DOWN

* 1 Age of 27
  2 Rumanian, Irish and Oriental leaders meet in city
* 3 It was wasted on Caroline
  4 Young Allan followed his young sister to find agave fiber
  5 The frozen lake — shoot the length of it
* 6 Parker's former employer
  8 Mixed lace found knotted with part of surrey is not sacred
*10 Poirot's cottage
  12 Confused game runs wild in distorted sin to provide mysteries

*14 Likely to be found in Caroline's Intelligence Corps
* 6 1's husband was one, as was 27's wife
*18 "Very prevalent in high society"
  21 Canada's leader at South Head was fearfully highminded about felines (3, 4)
*23 How 27 died
*25 King's _____
*27 Manufactured wagon wheels
  29 Crazy ant goes brown when hit
*31 Years Raymond had been at Fernly Park

Murder in Three Acts
(Three-Act Tragedy)

ACROSS

* 1 Appeared in *Lord Aintree's Dilemma*
* 4 An illegitimate child
* 7 Saw Bartholomew die
  8 Administrator to assess
  9 Concealed in Delhi department
*10 11's living
*11 One's title
 12 Tatar Gospel reveals Greek city
 13 French painter last seen in the part is terrible
 15 Puzzle-maker haunts bar and alley

*16 Owner of Ambrosine, Ltd.
*17 Rode in the Grand National
 18 Decapitate a crania
 19 Guillaume Augier drinks French water
 20 Repeatedly adamant, confuses sin awkwardly sits
 21 Brief and confused biography indicated sorcery
*22 Mr. Mugg's profession
 23 A mass mentioned a hoard

DOWN

* 1 Had alcoholic husband
  2 Master of Liberal Arts scrambles to make escape
  3 Odor is money, we hear!
* 4 Tollie bought this Abbey
  5 Ned tumbled to the conclusion
* 6 One of 4's employers
* 7 Address of Lord and Lady Eden
* 8 The Chief Constable
*10 Ellis may have left Melfort through this
*11 Father of Edward, Lloyd, Robin and Stephen

 13 Refers all mixed dues
*14 Muriel's profession
*15 Favorite haunt of Mr. Satterthwaite
*16 Mr. Satterthwaite's address
 17 In the middle of a fast, this uncle suggested a doctor
*18 Nicotine is used on them
 20 Is Rumania's leader containing the Jewish state?
 21 Torn dictionary reveals poem

Murder for Christmas
(Hercule Poirot's Christmas)

ACROSS

* 1 The Lee's "keep memory _____ "
* 3 According to his father, George was a pompous one
* 6 Stephen used a gramophone for his
* 7 AKA Conchita Lopez
*10 Horbury broke one
 12 Relieve lithic of its twitch to see school for studying Leigh Hunt
*15 Married one of David's friends
*16 Gorston Hall's cook
*17 One of 36's gardens represented Piana in _____

*21 Knew the value of central heating
*23 Where 7 kept her photographs
 24 Rover stumbles on messy pie to go past prime
 26 Sounds like the tea woman
 28 Refreshment sounds like good starting point
 30 Aram edict exposed doctor
 33 Meat mimicks cook, we hear!
*35 Where Stephen came to
*36 "An energetic, lean greyhound"

DOWN

 1 Leg dissolves into jelly
* 2 Present in Gorston Hall, according to 36
 3 Chinese dynasty echoes a path
 4 Academy in North America shields car union
 5 This animal sounds recent
* 6 Ran his father's business
 7 Dessert sounds mathematical
* 8 Stephen was initially excited by this
 9 Decline garbage
 10 Rail follows grain to find bird (4, 5)
*11 "Heavily, middle-aged men"
 13 Here lies buried in ancient Rome
*14 Her "frank and unsuspicious mind" led to her death

*18 "Died away in a choke or gurgle"
*19 Wanted to enjoy lost youth
*20 Profession of 15's husband
*22 7 was the "devil's _____ "
*23 15's maiden name
 25 To take abbreviated leave in France
*27 "All cats are _____ in the dark"
*29 36 likened herself to this gardener
 31 English artist hides this time
 32 In the name of God in ancient Rome
*34 One of 36's gardens represented this dead

Sad Cypress

ACROSS

* 1 Starred in film 7 saw at Alledore
* 4 Forbes _____ , Rycroft's home
* 8 Lady Rattery's brother
  9 The hazy air revealed a river mouth
 10 I stepped into the ice before the saint — we were the coldest
*11 Found scrap of label behind kitchen table
 12 I'm a partial genius — that's the picture!
*13 Nurse Hopkins could always do with this
*15 4 was never this
*16 "Girls are very artful" was in this
*18 Old Gerrard's wife's job
 19 Last will contains Sudanic language

*23 One of James Littledale's employers
*24 Left her money to Roddy
*25 Laura died in hers
 26 Deer exposed by poem!
*28 Natural mother of 6
 29 The way this Frenchman approached the crazy race was a comedy
*31 Laura's solicitor
 32 Fast river drowns three
*33 She put the kettle on
*34 The confectioner's assistant
 35 First woman joins New Testament — quite an occasion!

DOWN

* 1 Put morphine in sandwiches?
* 2 Roddy compared Mary to her
* 3 One was needed to cut Nurse O'Brien's brogue
* 4 Solved the Benedict Farley case
* 5 Cottage where Jessie lived
* 6 There was "a wild-rose unreality about her"
* 7 Worked at Henderson's garage
*14 Poirot's friend
*15 28 never made one
 17 Stop troop supplies short of the end

*19 In love with 6
 20 With little interest, the French duke picked up a small peg to see new recruit
*21 Mrs. Dacres left her money to one
*22 Namesake of 24
*23 Unexpectedly, he had a freckled face
*27 What they were going to do with Laura's body
*28 Where 6 lived
*30 Brought fresh milk twice a day

Evil Under the Sun

ACROSS

* 1 Where "the great cult of the Seaside for Holidays" was established
* 4 Author of *The Young Stepmother*
  9 Railroad blankets north, captures second navy
  10 District Attorney knocked out crazy Nat to release Indian
*12 Poirot's friend
*13 Kenneth's first wife's first husband ate it
 15 Accountant joined English artist in Ghanaian city
 17 Eegrruy — a chessy anagram
*19 Left all his money to Arlena
*21 Alice was found strangled on Blackridge _____

 22 Sounds as if she's a drug
 24 King and Emperor surround bishop to get baseball stat
 25 Old Latin falls behind new identity to discover recent film star (3, 4)
 27 Confused article points to short Ethiopian
*29 Blatt wanted to turn Leathercombe Bay "into a cross between _____ and Le Touquet"
 31 Yale and Lehi's leaders grip poem to release melody
*33 Poirot admired her "as much as any woman he had ever met"
*34 Police Surgeon at Pixie Cove

DOWN

* 1 What Mr. Gardener called his wife
* 2 *The Four Feathers* or *Vice* _____
  3 Don stumbles, but gives go-ahead
  5 The recital was reorganized to reveal object
* 6 Her mother died in childbirth
  7 Marijuana meal
* 8 Rosamund wouldn't like to be her
*11 Had "a penchant for making unfortunate marriages"
*14 Formerly at St. Helen's
*16 About Arlena's face there was a " _____ immobility"

 18 Sounds like you went to a disordered Iran haltingly to discover radioactive material
*20 Where 11 and 33 spent childhood
*21 14 walked from Leathercombe Bay to here
*23 "She had something that Arlena Marshall did not have. . . .Brains"
 26 We arrived before a drunken Ray, only to find ourselves tired
*28 AKA Arlena
 30 R sounds like L in brief religion
 32 A failure no matter which way you turn

Murder After Hours (The Hollow)

ACROSS

* 1 10 had a voice like one
  5 General Cyrano de Mobius conceals wish to disband army
  8 Young and confused Robert revealed a poetical eye
* 9 Poirot lived in one
  11 Deputy Chief Inspector discloses his rank
  12 Carlos' tiara hides Roman port
  14 Young Effie and confused Abel join in being expressive
*16 "Ascending Thought" was exhibited at the New _____
*18 The Angkatells were all so terribly _____
  20 Fifty enter race after less than a mile to provide wonder
*22 Nausicaa
  24 And all that sort of thing
*25 Henrietta had lived here
  27 Alpha image points direction
*28 Veronica said she needed matches for this
*30 Sir Henry was ex-governor of some
  32 The venerable but crazy Bede gripped this confusing bit, but the receding water swallowed them both (3, 4)
*33 Questioned the maids at The Hollow

DOWN

* 1 Poirot enjoyed a mid-morning cup of this
  2 Eve's beginning is a joke!
  3 One is made from this
* 4 Veronica's profession
* 5 What John didn't want to do
* 6 The poor relation
* 7 David was to go to this school in Athens
*10 Whitechapel Jewess
  13 Child and befuddled rodents are emblematic
*15 Sir Henry first met Poirot here
*17 Edward had been in the diplomatic _____
  19 Confusedly ordains to make forays
  21 Young Victor surrounded by Indians finds himself a hole
*23 She joined with Gudgeon to protect Lady Angkatell from her actions
*24 Wonderful in a crisis
  26 Nassau lich gate conceals council
  29 Dazed young Robert drops short musical term
  31 This one contains something new

Hickory, Dickory, Death
(Hickory, Dickory, Dock)

ACROSS

* 1 Mrs. Hubbard's sister
* 8 Worked for Mrs. Lucas
* 9 Black Bess
 10 A slot ax makes an instrument (4, 3)
*11 Studied on a Fulbrite
 13 Church of England struggles in morning to reach this height
*16 Hailed from Eire
*18 "The parsley sinking into the butter on a ＿＿ day"

*20 What 11 lost
 21 This knowledge betrays a humorist and a king
 22 I have
*24 8 had her passport
 28 A flower for rainbow goddess
*29 Lal and Ram were from here
*31 ＿＿ Fair
*32 Nigel favored this behavior
*34 Ring found in plate of soup
*35 Madame Mahmoudi's nationality

DOWN

 1 French and Swedish leaders surround two islands holding a justice to see islanders
 2 Lieutenant goes to harbor to get religious degree
 3 Yugoslavia's leader follows one hundred and one steamships to find effeminate Englishman
* 4 Had plumpers in her cheeks
* 5 "Supercilious and uncooperative"
* 6 Devoted to perfecting new filing system
* 7 This ink "would be even better" than green
 10 I am bored concealing this pulpit
 12 Path leading from shelter provides additional time
*14 Mrs. Hubbard shared these eyes with 1

*15 Was studying English
*16 One of stolen items made of this
*17 Collected pornography
 18 Man sounds a colorful cry
*19 Number of buses serving Hickory Road
*23 The Countess Rossakoff
 25 United States requires turbulent fuel to be serviceable
*26 Loathed English stew
*27 Part of Poirot's horizon, according to Colin
 28 In American northeast? That's ridiculous!
*29 ＿＿ , Olga, Nina, Gladys, Moira
 30 Young Albert and crazy Ned walk in English forest
 33 Attempt three, we hear!

The Clocks

ACROSS

* 1 Millicent went to a post office in this road
* 4 AKA Mrs. Hemming
* 9 Edwin Glen was this kind of photographer
*10 Of which Finn did 5 know?
*12 She didn't answer the telephone correctly
*13 Miss Martindale was this kind of cat
 14 Feet take a walk to arrive at festival
 17 Desire and drink filled five years
 18 Current returns to alter ms.

 21 School's leader joins now to discover narcotic
*23 What 31 taught
 26 I joined two beginners and the Yard's leader in feeling unwell
*27 Retired from a Cambridge Chair
*28 Given to Quentin before death
*31 Lived at 19 Wilbraham Crescent
 32 Lens reflects chartered accountant gripping frenzied fiddler
*33 Sheila's middle name
*34 Cafe near Cavendish Secretarial Bureau

DOWN

* 1 Mrs. Hemming's missing cat
* 2 Nigel's occupation
 3 Colony of wasps finds home in Cline Street
* 5 Christie author, client of Miss Martindale's
* 6 Tree in garden of 62 Wilbraham Crescent stands on its head
* 7 Building on Sheila's postcard
 8 Fly goes crazy to complete sonnet
 11 Woman is the same, however you look

*15 Family name of 12
*16 Gapp's stage name
*19 Real first name of 16
*20 Colin Lamb's assumed rank
*22 Chair at 19 Wilbraham Crescent
 23 English bank contains lutetium to give it color
*24 Mrs. Curtin lived in this street
*25 All the suspects required these
 29 Lamp upset, spilling oil
*30 Clocks read 13 minutes past this hour

The Moving Finger

ACROSS

1 Curtail supplying feathers
4 Speed was shown when the Father joined the Church of England
* 6 Lymstock looked as innocent as this garden
10 Arsenic makes this bird appear pale
*11 Complements blood, violence and 32
12 No sense of right or wrong found in a message
*13 Aimee's solicitor
*15 _____ Furze, Lymstock
*16 Mr. Pye's divine cook
*20 Barmaid at the Three Crowns
*22 Mrs. Dane Calthrop's guest
*25 Symmington's alleged relations with Miss Ginch
27 Many more requires mostly one more
*29 Symmington's partner
30 England's leader follows three confused wise men — you get the picture!
31 Teetotaler grips alternating current to show sense of touch
*32 "Trail of blood and violence and '11' and _____ "
33 Greek island rebuilds to stand tall

DOWN

* 1 "Helen of Troy had these _____ accents"
* 2 Location of 13's office
* 3 Anonymous letter pest may arise from this cause
* 4 Missing from Owen's dispensary
* 5 For Lymstock, Joanna should have been wearing this kind of jumper
7 Doctor of Engineering is just married to find natural religion
* 8 She wrote an advice column
9 These holy books are mostly confusing lies
14 180-degree jolt
*17 Where Agnes spent her childhood
18 Wood is mostly golfer's friend
*19 The Burtons' daily help
21 Peruvian Indian, Rabbi and Saint followed each other in autos (2, 4)
*23 Joanna's hairdresser
*24 _____ Mickford
25 Gold brick found in reversed coat
26 Flower found in Long Island and a French lake
*28 Jerry's doctor

A Murder is Announced

ACROSS

1 After death, just harmonize
4 Ape stumbles over seed
* 7 Assistant gardener at Dayas Hall
8 Sound of color in port
9 Eli followed a toad to a pickle shop (2, 1, 4)
10 Race covers much ground
*12 _____ Benham News and Chipping Cleghorn Gazette
13 The morning was confused for this scholar
14 A short time in charge of a twitch (1, 3)
15 Actress June belies much ruin
18 Ha! St. Elena reveals her speed
*20 5's rank
*21 _____ 27 Hotel
*22 7's husband supposedly killed here

23 Crazy Thea joined Alf to consume part (3, 4)
24 Best of Falla contains rubbish
*26 Wires were _____ using vase of water
29 Desirous glance given by British humorist, we hear!
*30 Initials of woman who was thirty years younger than her husband
*31 AKA Emma
33 Two scholars joined their mother
34 Northern air and magic come together in this city
*36 _____ Ashe, the gardener
*37 17's title
38 Child is the same, however you look
39 I, Guanajuato, ate a lizard

DOWN

1 A small apartment is likely
* 2 7's middle name
* 3 He wrote "tripey books"
* 4 Letitia always wore them
* 5 Interested in the psychology of murder
* 6 Mitzi's cake, Delicious _____
* 8 "Give me ducks every time," she said
*11 Julian Harmon's title
*13 Belle Goedler's nurse
*16 Charlotte went to him for a goiter operation

*17 Ex-Commissioner of Scotland Yard
19 Silk material produced in French city
24 To this end, I disagree
25 France's and Yalta's leaders climb bombed loft to view swastika
*27 Where Rudi formerly worked
*28 AKA Bunch
*32 "Life had been unkind" to her
35 I saw him holding Esau's young father

A Pocket Full of Rye

ACROSS

* 1 Name struck from family Bible
  3 Assistant looked around to discover thought
  6 Backward Bes continues haltingly to produce fat
*10 Percival met Jennifer while suffering from it
*11 She was a manicurist
*12 Discovered in Tanganyika
 13 I left Alaskan brown bears to find cameras
*15 Rex's physician
*17 Mr. Billingsley was this sort of man
*19 Where Percival was on holiday
 21 To receive veneration, I try Aldo, frenziedly
*24 He had "a pretty taste in suede shoes"
 25 Viewer wears a hat to protect camera (4, 3)
 29 The note on the television regained its place
*30 Gladys was this type
 31 To discover sound, I plunged into a turbulent scum
*32 Behead country where Lance lived
*33 Glady's boyfriend

DOWN

 1 Reverse downer does a flip
 2 Bread remade for Dutch commune
* 4 Miss Marple's cottage
 5 Unknown drinkers consume strange vaccine, achieving frigid state!
* 6 Jennifer probably had never heard of this term
* 7 " _____ with the Borgias"
* 8 Jennifer's " _____ and seems very stupid"
* 9 Adele's bedroom was furnished in this style
*14 What kind of piece was 11?
*15 " _____ of sixpence"
 16 Drug agent captures first person on steamship and us to find flower
*18 It was one thing, murder was another
*20 Rex was expecting these oil people
*22 Yewtree Lodge was 20 miles from here
*23 Rex suffered from General Paralysis of the _____
 26 Scoundrel receives note to see officers
*27 Pat's first husband was one
*28 Percival was " _____ and sly and cunning"

The Mirror Crack'd from Side to Side

ACROSS

* 1 "He hated music. Tone deaf, poor dear"
4 To see maiden, New Yorker takes speed
7 Pig's talk reveals tanning gum
* 8 Calmo "is prescribed for those under ____ "
9 Rodent is stuck in tar
*10 19 thought 5 a great one
*11 Mrs. Bantry's gardener
*12 Mrs. Jameson's professional name
13 Cheese crumbles on woman
14 And bathing resort goes French (2, 4)
15 Young Hyman and bewildered Sade bear five daughters
17 He reached battered Asti to guard hearth
18 "What ____ heart can gold despise? What cat's averse to fish?" — Thomas Gray
*19 Found prussic acid in her atomizer
*20 Much Benham *Herald &* ____
21 George Russell! O! Lust shields windy god
*22 His mother was killed in an accident
*23 She received the Gypsy's warning
*25 Originally from Huddersfield
26 Railroad gripping derailed train, exposing internal part
27 This one betrays time

DOWN

* 1 First husband of 5
2 This lid has been swallowed by that
3 Regarding the air, ventilate again
4 Metal melts to black in France
* 5 Bore a defective child
* 6 Secretary of the St. John's Ambulance Association
* 7 Returned to her former employer
* 8 Miss Marple's mead (2, 4)
10 Snake draws anger to reach high
*11 AKA Badcock
*13 Young Sandford's profession
*14 What sort of agent was 1?
*15 A body was found in the library at the ____
16 What you see is tall, we hear!
*17 Which ministry had purchased Gossington?
*18 Mr. Giles' occupation
*19 Lola married him after divorcing Rob
20 Meat minced to make Greek star
21 French milk spills on Gudrun's husband
23 This base solution is false, we hear!
*24 Griselda's husband, the former vicar

Caribbean Mystery

ACROSS

* 1 Raymond's wife
* 2 Mr. Rafiel sent them in code
* 5 Number of children Jim and Victoria had
* 7 8's people thought him undesirable
* 9 Kind of woman Molly's mother was
*11 Major Palgrave recognized him
12 Short Roman consumes spilled French milk
13 Vessel stores uranium and randon
14 Mineral water from distilled sap
*16 Raymond suggested a trip to them
18 Genetic molecule somersaults to conjunction
20 Alternately in ancient swastika
21 Erin deprived of land leaves anger behind

23 English painter defines his time
25 Three wise men taking a tumble is two-thirds of mystery
*28 Number of months between Greg's marriages
30 35 deserts Nadine, leaving behind continental institute
31 Sounds like this Indian likes to ease at the end of small creek
33 A drama unfolds, revealing a flotilla
*34 It's this sort of mystery
36 This day reserved for small fish, we hear!
*37 15 had one made of glass
*38 Belonged to the Valley of Death
*39 To Raymond, St. Mary Mead was scum on this

DOWN

* 1 Quarreled with wife in St. Mary Mead
* 3 Died in the bath
* 4 What Mr. Rafiel called Greg
* 5 Where "old hens" should go
6 Friend follows direction to find prisoner
* 8 Heard "voices in the bushes"
*10 Possible nationality of Greg
*11 Last thing Victoria held
12 Bostonian leaves town to find himself
*15 A photo was missing from his wallet

*17 Owing to 37, 15 couldn't do this well
*19 She was going to Trinidad
*22 Sign of the Horns averted this (4, 3)
24 Fish eggs are aligned by the sound of it
26 Fairy king stands on his head
*27 Nemesis wore one of pale pink
*29 A botanist interested in birds
*32 "Don't let's look for trouble," he warned
35 Man found in den

At Bertram's Hotel

ACROSS

1 French sweetener equals 100 centavos in Bolivian city

* 4 Former actress who worked at Bertram's

* 8 34 was generally considered to have packets of it

9 Adamant response contains obstruction

*10 To her, telephoning was "a shameful waste of money"

*11 18 was one of them

*12 He was only an agent

*13 One had one with six notches

*15 Her remodeled house had four flats

*16 "An ink stain round a mouse-hole" in this case

*18 "Quite a well known painter"

*19 Number of coal fires in Bertram's lounge

*23 Lady Selina thought Jane was this "years ago"

*24 This van was burgled

*25 Elvira's godfather

26 First half of missive gives clue to tennis call

*28 Jane's mother

29 Security found in safe type loses its head

*31 A groom and doorman

32 String to bind railway timber

*33 34 ran away with what kind of groom?

*34 Married Lord Coniston

*35 Johnnie Sedgwick could have used a few more of these

DOWN

* 1 Had been a member of the French Resistance

* 2 "Found much of his occupation tedious in the extreme"

* 3 The real one was in Yucatan

* 4 Ladislaus was this sort of driver

* 5 To what did Dr. Whittaker belong?

* 6 She was "sure to want to change her room"

* 7 Mr. Humphries was always taken to be him

14 Don deserts the castle keep

15 Pagoda door conceals ornamented wainscot

17 Young prophet saw wheel rolling

19 Alternately toddle

*20 One flew solo across it

*21 Robinson's partner

*22 Knew nothing, heard nothing, deduced little

*23 Brought Lady Selina Hazy to town

*27 Jane's great uncle

*28 Pennyfather's title

30 Shoe dismantled to discover stocking

The Seven Dials Mystery

ACROSS

* 1 AKA Eileen B. (6, 1)
  4 A city councilor used to be the defendant
* 7 Apparent cause of 23's death
  8 A shilling came between scholar and English artist in Iraqi capital
* 9 Superintendent Battle's department
*10 AKA Pongo
*11 23 was this
 12 Favored person will choose
*13 She owned dogs
*15 1's automobile

16 Louisiana horse is a straggler with Aramaic doctor
17 Sounds like a priory comes first (1, 6)
18 Garret for ancient Greek
19 I join Al to see fighter
20 In 501, Teresa concealed writer
21 A doughnut takes much fuss
*22 Negotiated with Eberhard at Wyvern Abbey
*23 He couldn't get up in the morning (5, 4)

DOWN

* 1 14's husband's first shop
  2 Diamond lady is same both ways
  3 Dazed runt got charred joining second grade
  4 A clam order suggests an outcry (1, 6)
  5 Relative always looks the same
* 6 The priory where Mrs. Coker lived
* 7 AKA George Lomax
  8 Restraining cover
*10 Her real name was Goldschmidt or Abrameier (1, 2, 4)
 11 Ace or TV — an excessive anagram

*13 "A real, genuine, blue-nosed automatic"
*14 "Rachel mourning for her children" (4, 5)
*15 Four o'clock
16 Neptune's trident is confusedly sterile
17 A gin gal conceals growing old
18 Order a slim light, we hear!
*20 The intruder escaped down this
21 Adams conceals Nabokov's woman

The Agatha Christie Title Hunt

DIRECTIVE

This puzzle consists of 4 parts. First, you must unscramble the following 50
Agatha Christie titles. Second, you must find the 50 titles in the letter grid.
Third, once you have successfully marked off all of the titles, the remaining
letters in the grid will spell out a 235-letter quotation concerning a famous
Christie character. (Read the quotation up and down the columns, beginning
from the bottom left, and transfer these letters to the spaces under the grid.)
Finally, with the 3 clues provided, you must discover who the quote is
about, who is speaking, and what book the quote is from.

SCRAMBLED TITLES

1 TAC EDR SUREHMB
2 HT TBAMTASL ORERE
3 BEU IHT ORGF
4 BCM TORULNOHA EEGE^t
5 TADNE CH RBE AOSTL
6 C YRATBNMRE ASIEAYB
7 APE CHIMA NTO TONGSEG
8 LES KHOCTC
9 DOORSHE COKEU
10 RANTUCI
11 MESL DOFA LANDY
12 ITCDO AT HED HUNESL^x
13 NHEIT TO NEL AHDE
14 TOKDANUIEOW SNTNINN^t
15 LUSONI DEB
16 WUTE MISDSNB
17 TEDSINS LEGNH
18 LAB TOLELN DEGH^o
19 RATONEALY WHELP
20 RORYCID COOKIKH YKCD^x
21 F DALORUR DEM HAIORY^x
22 WOE LOTHLH
23 THEOF NA UDODH*
24 POT RESHUEATM^o
25 CETRHI VT DUR AGAEMARE
26 PEATUN RE DOMORIIAMSM
27 ADIRET TU RENEM SHRC^t
28 SARSUM ED YEIR^x
29 TODLER SI RUM NENKH
30 ARESUD HES RIDM^x

31 SAT AHTYEIFART MEROYE SU TIFSLS_____
32 MEESINS_____
33 M OR N_____
34 BYT NUC ESOKOM WO LEHE^x_____
35 BIONCA DO YERELENCN_____
36 HAT ELOS REHEP_____
37 RATARSOFT EN SEGUPRNFK_____
38 LAPET DO RES INUEH_____
39 FOTANET PO SERF_____
40 MADETERREM DEBEH^t_____
41 RET CAVESA RERSHEDTY_____
42 NIT HOMEYS CR ETHECFES_____
43 SET NIVAS HYSEY LEMEDRT_____
44 TES DYSITHAFE RORYTMT^x_____
45 REMESERI LUPDGN^t_____
46 DIE TINSI TETLANN^t_____
47 DIRTE AS E IHTE_____
48 LIDRT RHIG_____
49 ROEWTAZ RODS^x_____
50 DET DEURH NGO^o_____

t – U.S. title is different
x – U.K. title is different
* – Published in U.K. only
o – Published in U.S. only

CLUES

1 OWNED A LARGE TURNIP-FACED WATCH_____
2 WAS EMPLOYED AS A PRIVATE SECRETARY_____
3 GEORGES CONNEAU COMMITTED MURDER_____

```
H I C K O R Y D I C K O R Y D O C K Y S A E S I R E D R U M
E S R O H E L A P E H T D E A D M A N S F O L L Y N T E E U
I M K Y R E T S Y M D R O F A T T I S E H T D A T D H D R R
F U E C N E C O N N I Y B L A E D R O N E F A N H L E R H D
T R H E O D E S A S M L R I G D R I H T N O H A E E M U T E
H D C M A L N I S N A I D N I E L T T I L N E T A S O M A R
G E N U E C C D W E Y O F D I W A S A W C R E T B S U G E I
A R I R H A O E E X R U O I O M W T F B N N H H C N S N D N
C A R D S O N T H E T A B L E M R N I M A E D E M I E I F M
A T R E D T O E H T A S L G Y U E E D U R A N S U G T P O E
R T U R G H T E N C T O R N C E H A N D A T I E R H R E D S
I H O S O E E Y E I H T E S U O H D E K O O R C D T A E N O
B E F H D G L E H E I E S U O H D N E T A L I R E P P L U P
B V T E R O T S H T D E A T H O N T H E N I L E R P E S O O
E I A S E L Y T S T A R I A F F A S U O I R E T S Y M E H T
A C T A D D T T W E L A I R E D R U M R O F Y A D I L O H A
N A B I N E I H N D I C A I T N I S E L B U O D E A D R R M
M R E D U N L A E Y R E T S Y M S L A I D N E V E S E H T I
Y A R S E B A T T R U F K N A R F O T R E G N E S S A P E A
S G T E H A D S E S M S Y E N M I H C F O T E R C E S E H T
T E R G T L E H R T F H E E T A F F O N R E T S O P R A O R
E V A G E L I O G I S D U O L C E H T N I H T A E D O W U H
R E M E M B E R E D D E A T H N E T A I E N K R T S A O W I
Y E S K N I L E H T N O R E D R U M D E P E Y Y U R F N D S
I F H S P H A L L O W E E N P A R T Y D P S N B D G N D O G
N W O N K N U N O I T A N I T S E D E D I T A S I E R E H T
C A T A M O N G T H E P I G E O N S D I A S Z B L S M M H O
E E E H A R R N E F M U R D E R I N T H R E E A C T S R T D
E U L C G N A R E M O O B E H T S A N N R H A S O I O E O S
H E E O H S Y M E L K C U B O W T E N O T O F S I S E M E N
```

———— ———— ———— ———— ——————,
———-———— ———— ———————— —
—————— —— ——— ————, ———— ————
————— ————— ———— —— ————
————————, ————— ————————
—————————, ——— —— ————————
———————! —— ——— ————— ———
—————————— —— —————————. ———
————————— —— ——— ———— —— ——— ——
————————— ————————…——————
——— ———————— ———— ——— ————.

The Parker Pyne Word Find

DIRECTIVE

The following puzzle is certain to test your knowledge of the perspicacious Mr. Parker Pyne, the detective who also introduced us to Miss Felicity Lemon — who went on to become Hercule Poirot's maddeningly efficient secretary — and to Ariadne Oliver — Agatha Christie's famous mystery authoress. This puzzle is basically a word find in which you must locate the names of 60 characters, the titles of 12 Parker Pyne short stories and a hidden message. The titles of the stories are provided. Beneath them are clues from which you will be able to determine the names of the characters that you will be looking for in the letter grid. Once you have looped all of the titles and the names, you will be left with a number of letters, which will reveal Parker Pyne's famous advertisement. Read the letters in a linear fashion — left to right — and transfer them to the spaces provided under the grid.

CLUES

THE MIDDLE-AGED WIFE
1 George Packingham's gold-digging clerk (5)_____
2 From "model of economy" to spendthrift (5, 10)_____
3 Wanted terribly to be young (6, 10)_____

THE DISCONTENTED SOLDIER
1 Vacuum Gas clerk (5, 5)_____
2 Assaulted Freda Clegg (5)_____
3 Novelist and Pyne staff member (6)_____
4 Jerry's partner (5)_____
5 Soldier back from East Africa, he liked anemic women (9)_____

THE DISTRESSED LADY
1 In the dark with Jules (5, 10)_____
2 Much taken with Sanchia (6)_____
3 Claude Luttrell's pseudonym (5)_____
4 "Invested in a La Merveilleuse transformation," Pyne said (9)_____
5 With Jules, created furor in Paris (7)
6 Secretary to Lady Naomi, pseudonym of Ernestine (6)_____

THE DISCONTENTED HUSBAND
1 Also afflicted with athletic husband who talked stocks (10)_____
2 Culture-mad, her husband claimed (4)_____
3 The inarticulate type, he had inferiority complex (8, 4)_____

85

THE CITY CLERK

1 Military appearance and bovine face, Pyne friend (5)_____
2 Bestowed Order of St. Stanislaus on Mr. Roberts (4)_____
3 Felt he was "in the middle of one of his favorite novels" (7)_____
4 Fourth daughter of hard-working Streatham family (6, 6)_____
5 A tall old gentleman and Pyne employee, played Count (4)_____

THE RICH WOMAN

1 Pyne associate, spiked Amelia's coffee with hemp (8)_____
2 Pseudonym of Dr. Antrobus (1, 11)_____
3 Cornish farm woman, Pyne saved her only son (7)_____
4 Amelia's adopted personality (6)_____
5 Wealthy widow (5)_____
6 Good-humored farm hand, Amelia got him off drink (3)_____

HAVE YOU GOT EVERYTHING YOU WANT?

1 Rigorous puritanism his problem (6)_____
2 American wife to Edward (5)_____
3 Edward and Elsie (8)_____
4 Stopped train with smoke bomb (8)_____

THE GATE OF BAGDAD

1 "Never knew how far the English were serious" (4)_____
2 Had "thirst for Biblical knowledge" (5)_____
3 Frivolous niece of stern aunt (5)_____
4 Defaulting financier and great criminal (4)_____
5 Quiet man, belonged to Bagdad public works department (7)_____
6 Squadron leader and Air Force doctor (6)_____
7 Armenian on tour (9)_____

THE HOUSE AT SHIRAZ

1 Mad as a hatter, went completely native (4)_____
2 Ladies' maid, beloved of Herr Schlagal (4)_____
3 Sentimental German and airplane pilot (8)_____

THE PEARL OF PRICE

1 Prosperous magnate or "purse-proud hog" (5)_____
2 Lost earring reputedly worth $40,000 (5)_____
3 Elderly archeologist (6)_____
4 Gallant Frenchman, possessed fine Gallic cynicism (6)_____
5 Blundell's secretary and former thief (3)_____
6 Tired-looking Englishman and MP (6)_____

DEATH ON THE NILE

1 "Nunks," had been "treated like a worm for ten years" (6)_____
2 Nobody ever snapped at him (4)_____
3 Suffered "from the complaint of having too much money" (6)_____
4 Lady Ariadne's nurse, relied on own judgment (5)_____
5 Grieved that Parker Pyne missed Temple of Abdyos (8)_____

THE ORACLE AT DELPHI

1 Widow, her spiritual home was Riviera, not Greece (6)_____
2 Spectacled kidnap victim (7, 2)_____

NAMES APPEARING IN SEVERAL STORIES

1 Forbidding-looking young woman, Pyne's secretary (4, 5)_____
2 "Queen of the Vamps" and Pyne employee (9, 2, 4)_____
3 "Lounge Lizard" employed by Pyne (6, 8)_____
4 The detective's first name and usual form of address (2, 6)_____
5 The detective's last name (4)_____

```
H U S B A N D A T N A W U O Y G N I H T Y R E V E
D T H E D I S T R E S S E D L A D Y N A M O W H T
E T A E S U O H E H T C T H E O R A C L E A T C O
T S N O T G N I S S A M N O M E L S S I M N D I G
N H R L E H G E O R G E E L Y A R G R E Y A E R U
E I Y O L A L E V R A M P E T E R S A E O N L E O
T R M F S N R E M I E H T R O D I M O A N C P H Y
N A E T I N R F U D E M M A H O M J E R R Y H T E
O Z R U E A H A R S U B A Y S K A U P E L S I E V
C E P S B H Y ? P E N T E M I A N L I F N N O D A
S C A R R E C Y R P D J E F F R I E S P O L I A H
I I R I S A N C H I A A C A L E B S N E T T A D E
D R P T C N O T G N I K C A P E G R O E G O N G L
E P A N T R O B U S S U L L T M G A R D N E R A I
H F U R P A E N I T S E N R E C A R O L I R W B N
T O L E N I T N A T S N O C C G K E R P K Y E F E
C L A U D E L U T T R E L L O N G N L U C A S O H
A R A S E D E N I E L E D A M E E N H P A D T E T
K A 17 R I W I L L A R D J R C R E K R A P R M T N
R E L A G A L H C S S R E Y A S E I G G A M I A O
E P Y N E R Y E L S N E H M A H A R B L I W J G H
L E H M O D U B O S C S T R E B O R Y C R E P E T
C H R E G I N A L D W A D E R E V I L O A N D H A
Y T I C E H T E F I W D E G A E L D D I M E H T E
R E I D L O S D E T N E T N O C S I D E H T S T D
```

___ ___ _____? __ ___, _____
__. _____ ____, __ _____ __.

The Harley Quin Word Find

DIRECTIVE

Like the harlequin figure from the Renaissance *commedia dell' arte* and the harlequin of the early English stage, Harley Quin possessed magical powers. Together with Mr. Satterthwaite, through whom Harley Quin enacted his powers, he appeared in 14 Agatha Christie short stories, all but 2 of which appeared in a single collection. In this word find you must locate 76 names, the titles of 13 of the Harley Quin short stories and a hidden message. The titles of the stories are provided. Beneath them are the clues from which you will be able to determine the names that you will be looking for on the letter grid. Once you have looped the titles and the names, you will be left with a number of letters, which will reveal the titles of both the American and English editions of the Harley Quin stories. Read the letters from left to right and transfer them to the spaces provided under the grid.

CLUES

THE HARLEQUIN TEA SET

1 Color-blind and gout-ridden (6)_____
2 Waiter at Harlequin Cafe (3)_____
3 "Guards the ricks and guards the hay" (6, 6)_____
4 Simon's second wife (5)_____
5 Still astrally present (4)_____
6 Roly (6)_____
7 Ex-squadron leader (5)_____
8 The actual heir (7)_____
9 Reliable and devoted to his daughter (2, 6)_____
10 Beloved of Timothy and Roland (4)_____
11 Lily's sister (5)_____
12 Bore Quin's last message (6)_____
13 Hermes' owner (6, 4)_____

THE COMING OF MR. QUIN

1 Present when Capel shot himself (7)_____
2 "Serious political wife" (5)_____
3 Suspected wife of murder (4)_____
4 Acquitted but haunted by suspicion (7)_____
5 Purchased Royston (3)_____
6 Quin's unobtrusive monkey's paw (13)_____

THE SHADOW ON THE GLASS

1 Saved Cynthia from dying of boredom in Cairo (5)_____
2 Social director (5)_____
3 "All sunburn and silence" (6)_____
4 Shot dead in Privy Garden at Greenways (5)_____
5 Possessed "a manner that radiated magnetism" (5)_____
6 "The sort of woman who'd stick at nothing" (4)_____
7 Owner of Greenways (3)_____

8 Bothered by ghost (8)_____
9 "Shrewd-looking, forceful man of forty-odd" (9)_____

AT THE BELLS AND MOTLEY

1 Proprietor of Bells and Motley (7)_____
2 "Canadian and a stranger" (7)_____
3 Ashley Grange gardener (7)_____
4 Disappearing husband (7)_____
5 Worked in father's inn (4, 5)_____

THE SIGN IN THE SKY

1 Tracked to Banff (6, 7)_____
2 "Perhaps a tiny bit stupid" (6, 4)_____
3 Gave Louisa a job (6)_____
4 Owned murder weapon (6)_____

THE SOUL OF THE CROUPIER

1 "Doing Europe in a stern and conscientious spirit" (9)_____
2 Dressed like "a glorified bird of paradise" (9)_____
3 "Curious mixture of native shrewdness and idealism" (5)_____
4 Countess Czarnova (6)_____
5 Absinthe made his heart grow fonder (6)_____

THE WORLD'S END

1 Her face "just missed being beautiful" (5)_____
2 Did not steal opal (6)_____
3 Cut up food for his wife (4)_____
4 Much-married actress (4)_____
5 Retired judge (9)_____
6 Had "very white face and very black hair" (4)_____

THE VOICE IN THE DARK

1 Was on *Uralia* when it went down (6)_____
2 On his way to becoming a fifth husband (5)_____
3 Ladies' maid? (5)_____
4 In love with curate (4)_____
5 Very keen on horses (6)_____
6 "The most wonderful medium that ever existed" (5)_____
7 Heir to title after Margery (5)_____
8 Her hobbies were getting married (4)_____

THE FACE OF HELEN

1 Thought by Mr. Satterthwaite a very ordinary young man (5)_____
2 Glass blower (4)_____
3 Music student and unconscious siren (4)_____

THE DEAD HARLEQUIN

1 Painted Dead Harlequin (5)_____
2 "Like a ghost herself" (4)_____
3 Introduced Satterthwaite and Bristow (4)_____
4 Charnley governess (4)_____
5 Impersonator (4)_____
6 Wept and carried Silver Ewer (4)_____

THE BIRD WITH THE BROKEN WING

1 Youngest of "ill-fated Clydesleys" (7)_____
2 Had determined laugh (5)_____
3 Aspiring young medium (4)_____

4 Ouijah spirit control (3)_____
5 Thought Mr. Satterthwaite "rather a duck" (5)_____
6 Were no messages on board for her (5)_____
7 Wore "a hungry despairing look" (8)_____

THE MAN FROM THE SEA

1 Regretted never having fathered son (6)_____
2 White house, La _____ (3)_____

HARLEQUIN'S LANE

1 No one would have guessed her foreign background (3)_____
2 Forced wife to choose between career and him (4)_____
3 Pierette (5)_____

```
I N G I S E H T E S A E T N I U Q E L R A H E H T
N E L E H F O E C A F E H T Z E N I A E S E H T M
T H E B I R D W I T H T H E B R O K E N W I N G O
H E R M E S T O M L I N S O N A M N E D N A L O R
E R O N A E L E I M O A N H W E S T T O C S H P F
S E A N N E S L E Y E L A D A I V L Y S A E T A N
K I I M I R A B E L L E T G E R A R D T M L E Z A
Y P R H D R A L L U B A S I U O L E T P A L B K M
N U A I A U A J A S M S S A R A H E S I D E A R E
I O M L S D C O D S O N A H N D R G Y O G B Z A H
U R E R N G F H Y M L R I A R T O Q U Q E A I D T
Q C N O U E I N N T L U H R H G H R E M U M L E Y
R E A N N O R R A B Y B T W M A R C I A N I E H E
M H L A N Y S D R A G E A E A L I C E S K D N T L
F T S E Y P O R T E R I M L N E L G T E E L E N T
O F N L E F R A N K T R D L I B A B S N R E N I O
G O I E L J O H N E O E Y N I T R A M O T I U E M
N L U F O R D C O B B R O O B M I B P J O F S C D
I U Q J R B X I L A S R L T I M O T H Y N K A I N
M O E E Y E L R A B Y E L R A H M A I R V N M O A
O S L A A R M A I L L I W O M R Q R L A Y I O V S
C E R N D Y M M I J U P I H N D D U J M S W H E L
E H A N A L I N I U Q E L R A H D A E D E H T H L
H T H E W O R L D S E N D D M O T L N O M I S T E
T H E S H A D O W O N T H E G L A S S A T T H E B
```

___ _____ __ __, ____
___ _____ __, ____

Murder at the Vicarage Kriss-Kross

DIRECTIVE

The following kriss-kross (a numberless and formless grid) tests your
detection skills in two ways. In the traditional kriss-kross you are provided
with a number of words, grouped by length, which you must fit on a grid.
The twist here is that in order to arrive at your word list you must first
answer the clues, all of which are drawn from *Murder at the Vicarage*, and
then put them in their appropriate places on the grid.

CLUES

3 LETTERS

1 ———— Hall

4 LETTERS

1 She was in love with Lawrence Redding
2 Dr. Stone's secretary
3 A St. Mary Mead gossip
4 Attended the inquest
5 Lucius Protheroe's parlor maid

5 LETTERS

1 Mary ————
2 Mrs. Price Ridley's maid
3 St. Mary Mead's new curate
4 Martha ———— Ridley
5 "Rude and overbearing" inspector
6 An imposter
7 Leonard Clement's title

6 LETTERS

1 Lived next to Miss Marple
2 Lawrence Redding's housekeeper
3 Destined for merchant marine
4 ———— Cram
5 Village magistrate
6 Victim of threatening phone call
7 Colonel Protheroe's butler
8 Martha Price ————
9 Mr. Hawes's landlady

7 LETTERS

1 Dr. Roberts's job
2 Held after Colonel Protheroe's death
3 Married a younger woman
4 Mrs. Lestrange's daughter

5 In love with Anne Protheroe_____

6 Oversaw inquest_____

7 Housekeeper at Old Hall_____

8 LETTERS

1 A mixture of "vinegar and gush"_____

2 "Much dreaded by the poor"_____

3 "A clever painter"_____

4 Colonel Protheroe's cook (3, 5)_____

5 Lived next to Amanda Hartnell_____

9 LETTERS

1 Miss Marple's physician (2, 7)_____

2 A "pompous old brute"_____

10 LETTERS

1 Town 2 miles from St. Mary Mead (4, 6)_____

2 "A stagnant pool" (2, 4, 4)_____

11 LETTERS

1 "A brilliant novelist" (7, 4)_____

12 LETTERS

1 "Mysterious lady of St. Mary Mead" (3, 9)_____

14 LETTERS

1 "Nasty old cat" (4, 4, 6)_____

2 First officer at scene of crime (9, 5)_____

15 LETTERS

1 22 years younger than husband (8, 7)_____

19 LETTERS

1 First Miss Marple novel (6, 2, 3, 8)_____

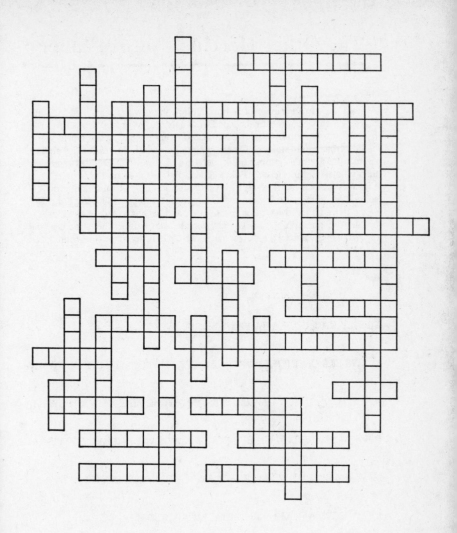

93

The Other Hercule Poirot Cipher

DIRECTIVE

At least once in the career of Hercule Poirot, there was a man who took his place, a man who almost succeeded in deceiving not only Poirot's dear friend Captain Arthur Hastings, but also the one woman in the world who held Poirot's attentions, the Countess Vera Rossakoff. The following cipher reveals the dramatic confrontation between Hastings, the Countess and the man who would be Hercule Poirot. The cipher is based on the famous Vigenère table, a multiple-alphabet substitution cipher, and to help you solve it we give you this clue to the keyword, taken from *The Big Four*: He was a twin, he lived near Spa in Belgium, and he possessed "a singularly indolent disposition" (7, 6). The keyword is then written above the cipher below, being repeated a sufficient number of times to cover the whole text.

CIPHER

TJL ULY FTGQUS FE YHA YZX WSZTIEE RVQCZX.

WS ERG OETF TTVI WWU, VLMRCVZOTRPFQCM EIML PTX. XWSZV

KTS VOM DLQT SOX-GAARLL SPES, HPV GTMG ZBCFXIWVX TBGWYM,

OPPXQIKSEY RSCXA. FJH BYS OOKJM HLW SWNWSKEPA, IYN XWS

MPSL IPZBPLH DT JVWGG IYMPY ATFM UOKK, CUL DFVTZG KVX

MQBAELGWSA — KVHSG MIXZYH AWLGMAEOMD — ?

XC GSNCSVTKVVD HIGS KLH LHQYB MJ XWS KFIGTGZA'D GSXQM.

JVX SVLXAPH UCZNOKD, JLZ GZMRS ZZBZIPN ETEL TLKZHXMGUB.

"JZY WODV PXEP KMNPMKSL. KVTT OHV TD RDH PVFVUNL XZTVDH!"

DIRECTIVE FOR VIGENÈRE TABLE

The alphabet running across the top is called the clear alphabet, while the one running down the left side is known as the key alphabet. To decipher a message using this table, you must find the key letter (derived from the keyword, in the key alphabet), run across the corresponding row until you locate the letter you wish to decipher, and then look up to find the deciphered letter in the clear alphabet.

THE VIGENÈRE TABLE

```
    A B C D E F G H I J K L M N O P Q R S T U V W X Y Z
A   A B C D E F G H I J K L M N O P Q R S T U V W X Y Z
B   B C D E F G H I J K L M N O P Q R S T U V W X Y Z A
C   C D E F G H I J K L M N O P Q R S T U V W X Y Z A B
D   D E F G H I J K L M N O P Q R S T U V W X Y Z A B C
E   E F G H I J K L M N O P Q R S T U V W X Y Z A B C D
F   F G H I J K L M N O P Q R S T U V W X Y Z A B C D E
G   G H I J K L M N O P Q R S T U V W X Y Z A B C D E F
H   H I J K L M N O P Q R S T U V W X Y Z A B C D E F G
I   I J K L M N O P Q R S T U V W X Y Z A B C D E F G H
J   J K L M N O P Q R S T U V W X Y Z A B C D E F G H I
K   K L M N O P Q R S T U V W X Y Z A B C D E F G H I J
L   L M N O P Q R S T U V W X Y Z A B C D E F G H I J K
M   M N O P Q R S T U V W X Y Z A B C D E F G H I J K L
N   N O P Q R S T U V W X Y Z A B C D E F G H I J K L M
O   O P Q R S T U V W X Y Z A B C D E F G H I J K L M N
P   P Q R S T U V W X Y Z A B C D E F G H I J K L M N O
Q   Q R S T U V W X Y Z A B C D E F G H I J K L M N O P
R   R S T U V W X Y Z A B C D E F G H I J K L M N O P Q
S   S T U V W X Y Z A B C D E F G H I J K L M N O P Q R
T   T U V W X Y Z A B C D E F G H I J K L M N O P Q R S
U   U V W X Y Z A B C D E F G H I J K L M N O P Q R S T
V   V W X Y Z A B C D E F G H I J K L M N O P Q R S T U
W   W X Y Z A B C D E F G H I J K L M N O P Q R S T U V
X   X Y Z A B C D E F G H I J K L M N O P Q R S T U V W
Y   Y Z A B C D E F G H I J K L M N O P Q R S T U V W X
Z   Z A B C D E F G H I J K L M N O P Q R S T U V W X Y
```

The Poisoner's Word Grid
& Match-Up

DIRECTIVE

In this puzzle you are presented with a grid (on the opposite page) containing 77 letters, which you will need to spell the names of 11 poisons used in Agatha Christie's books. Each letter has a numerical value, which is determined by adding together the numbers of both the row and the column in which the letter is found. The number 6, for instance, may be arrived at by adding together 1 and 5, 5 and 1, 3 and 3, 4 and 2, or 2 and 4. You must decide which combination of numbers provides you with the letters needed to spell out each of the poisons in the column below. Once you have deciphered the poisons, transfer your answers to the second column on the following page and proceed to match the poisons with their victims, means of administration and the books in which they appeared.

1	2	6	7	9	7	11	12
2	4	4	8	12	11	13	14
3	6	15	11	13	17	9	5
4	7	14	8	4	14	10	10
5	7	6	9	10	12	12	17
6	12	10	8	15	12	9	8
7	8	16	13	18	8	13	16
8	13	16	10	8	6	11	14
9	6	11	11	5	7	9	11
10	13	5	15	3	5	3	10
11	10	9	7	9	12	15	14

	1	2	3	4	5	6	7
1	H	A	R	C	A	R	O
2	N	C	H	S	O	E	A
3	A	O	E	C	E	I	E
4	T	H	R	A	L	U	I
5	A	M	V	P	E	X	N
6	E	S	D	Y	I	A	C
7	N	O	O	C	H	E	A
8	L	N	S	I	R	C	N
9	M	T	C	A	I	I	R
10	N	R	P	E	C	E	L
11	K	T	S	R	L	N	O

VICTIM	POISON	MEANS	BOOK
CHARLES CRADDOCK	_____	OVERDOSE	THE MURDER OF ROGER ACKROYD
GEORGE BARTON	_____	SHAVING BRUSH	CROOKED HOUSE
ELLA ZIELINSKY	_____	SUICIDE	THE SEVEN DIALS MYSTERY
AMYAS CRALE	_____	TEA	MURDER IN RETROSPECT (FIVE LITTLE PIGS)
ARISTIDE LEONIDES	_____	ATOMIZER	SAD CYPRESS
ALFRED CRACKENTHORPE	_____	SANDWICH	CARDS ON THE TABLE
COCO COURTENEY	_____	TABLETS	REMEMBERED DEATH (SPARKLING CYANIDE)
MRS. FERRARS	_____	WHISKY	WHAT MRS. MCGILLICUDDY SAW! (4:50 FROM PADDINGTON)
HAROLD CRACKENTHORPE	_____	BEER	"THE AFFAIR AT THE VICTORY BALL"
MARY GERRARD	_____	WINE	THE MIRROR CRACK'D FROM SIDE TO SIDE
GERRY WADE	_____	INSULIN	WHAT MRS. MCGILLICUDDY SAW! (4:50 FROM PADDINGTON)

The Miss Marple Quotefall

DIRECTIVE

In this puzzle you are to fit the letters in each column into the boxes directly above the letters in order to form words, which will read from left to right. The letters may or may not go into the boxes in the same order in which they are given. You must decide which letter goes in which box above it. Once a letter is used, cross it off the bottom half of the diagram and do not use it again. A black square indicates the end of a word. When you are finished, you will have a searing observation on life by one of Agatha Christie's most famous sleuths, and the name of that person.

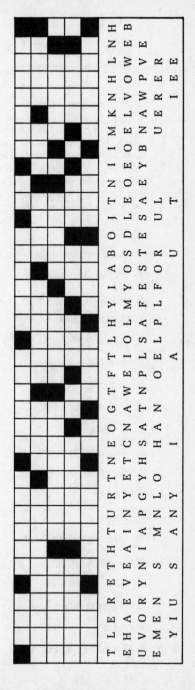

The Case of the Noted Nephew: An Agatha Christie Double Crostic

DIRECTIVE

Within the Agatha Christie canon lurks one of the most famous nephews in all detective fiction. Often ascerbic in his observations, he was nonetheless filled with love for his aging aunt. In this puzzle you are to find the occupation of this nephew, his name, and a 134-letter quotation relating to him. To do so you must first answer the clues A through S. The first letter of each of the answers will spell out the nephew's occupation and name. Then, if you transfer each of the letters of the answers to the appropriately lettered and numbered squares on the answer grid, you will be able to read something to your advantage.

CLUES

A Argument about age

$\overline{13}$ $\overline{23}$ $\overline{60}$ $\overline{69}$ $\overline{81}$ $\overline{88}$ $\overline{107}$ $\overline{15}$

B Flattened at the poles

$\overline{63}$ $\overline{74}$ $\overline{90}$ $\overline{92}$ $\overline{96}$ $\overline{98}$

C Designed to hold water

$\overline{112}$ $\overline{113}$ $\overline{114}$ $\overline{117}$ $\overline{132}$ $\overline{21}$

D Artist's frames

$\overline{26}$ $\overline{79}$ $\overline{93}$ $\overline{102}$ $\overline{103}$ $\overline{122}$

E Attempted to influence bill

$\overline{129}$ $\overline{5}$ $\overline{43}$ $\overline{83}$ $\overline{111}$ $\overline{6}$ $\overline{64}$

F Secreted in the pancreas

$\overline{68}$ $\overline{95}$ $\overline{123}$ $\overline{128}$ $\overline{130}$ $\overline{2}$ $\overline{30}$

G Lazy

$\overline{41}$ $\overline{51}$ $\overline{72}$ $\overline{116}$ $\overline{19}$ $\overline{22}$ $\overline{33}$ $\overline{54}$ $\overline{55}$

H Between 13 and 19

$\overline{86}$ $\overline{91}$ $\overline{104}$ $\overline{108}$ $\overline{121}$ $\overline{126}$ $\overline{12}$

I Enraptures

$\overline{27}$ $\overline{82}$ $\overline{11}$ $\overline{18}$ $\overline{28}$ $\overline{32}$ $\overline{44}$ $\overline{73}$

J Increases the sound

$\overline{94}$ $\overline{7}$ $\overline{17}$ $\overline{45}$ $\overline{46}$ $\overline{61}$ $\overline{124}$ $\overline{47}$ $\overline{78}$

K Canadian territory

$\overline{70}$ $\overline{85}$ $\overline{77}$ $\overline{84}$ $\overline{125}$

L Money

$\overline{34}$ $\overline{75}$ $\overline{76}$ $\overline{101}$ $\overline{105}$

M Busy

$\overline{115}$ $\overline{38}$ $\overline{58}$ $\overline{87}$ $\overline{89}$ $\overline{29}$ $\overline{49}$ $\overline{106}$

N Cleaning fluid, solvent

$\overline{131}$ $\overline{10}$ $\overline{97}$ $\overline{1}$ $\overline{24}$ $\overline{36}$ $\overline{16}$

O Famines

$\overline{127}$ $\overline{52}$ $\overline{20}$ $\overline{66}$ $\overline{25}$ $\overline{39}$ $\overline{133}$

P Once upon a time

$\overline{35}$ $\overline{71}$ $\overline{37}$ $\overline{110}$ $\overline{14}$ $\overline{62}$

Q Begins at sunset

$\overline{65}$ $\overline{48}$ $\overline{53}$ $\overline{57}$ $\overline{40}$ $\overline{67}$ $\overline{109}$

R A fan

$\overline{134}$ $\overline{118}$ $\overline{120}$ $\overline{4}$ $\overline{99}$ $\overline{119}$ $\overline{31}$ $\overline{59}$ $\overline{80}$

S Founder of tragic drama

$\overline{50}$ $\overline{9}$ $\overline{56}$ $\overline{3}$ $\overline{100}$ $\overline{42}$ $\overline{8}$

1 N	2 F	3 S		4 R	5 E	6 E	7 J	8 S		
9 S	10 N	11 I	12 H		13 A	14 P		15 A	16 N	17 J	18 I	19 G	20 O	21 C
	22 G	23 A	24 N	25 O	26 D	27 I	28 I		29 M	30 F		31 R	32 I	33 G
34 L		35 P	36 N	37 P	38 M	39 O		40 Q	41 G		42 S		43 E	44 I
45 J	46 J	47 J	48 Q	49 M		50 S	51 G	52 O		53 Q	54 G	55 G	56 S	57 Q
58 M	59 R		60 A	61 J		62 P	63 B	64 E	65 Q	66 O	67 Q	68 F	69 A	70 K
	71 P	72 G	73 I		74 B	75 L	76 L	77 K	78 J		79 D	80 R	81 A	
82 I	83 E	84 K	85 K	86 H		87 M	88 A	89 M	90 B	91 H	92 B	93 D	94 J	95 F
96 B		97 N	98 B	99 R	100 S	101 L	102 D		103 D	104 H	105 L	106 M	107 A	108 H
109 Q		110 P	111 E	112 C	113 C	114 C		115 M	116 G		117 C	118 R	119 R	120 R
121 H	122 D	123 F	124 J	125 K	126 H		127 O	128 F	129 E	130 F	131 N	132 C	133 O	134 R

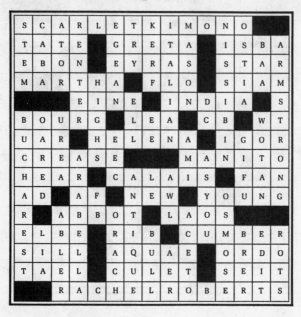

S	C	A	R	L	E	T	K	I	M	O	N	O	O	■
T	A	T	E	■	G	R	E	T	A	■	I	S	B	A
E	B	O	N	■	E	Y	R	A	S	■	S	T	A	R
M	A	R	T	H	A	■	F	L	O	■	S	I	A	M
■	■	E	I	N	E	■	I	N	D	I	A	■	■	S
B	O	U	R	G	■	L	E	A	■	C	B	■	W	T
U	A	R	■	H	E	L	E	N	A	■	I	G	O	R
C	R	E	A	S	E	■	■	M	A	N	I	T	O	■
H	E	A	R	■	C	A	L	A	I	S	■	F	A	N
A	D	■	A	F	■	N	E	W	■	Y	O	U	N	G
R	■	A	B	B	O	T	■	L	A	O	S	■	■	■
E	L	B	E	■	R	I	B	■	C	U	M	B	E	R
S	I	L	L	■	A	Q	U	A	E	■	O	R	D	O
T	A	E	L	■	C	U	L	E	T	■	S	E	I	T
■	R	A	C	H	E	L	R	O	B	E	R	T	S	■

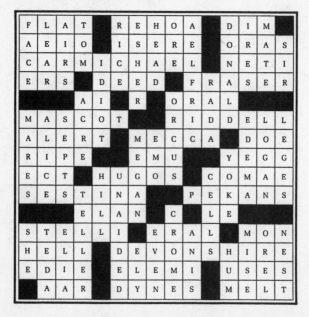

F	L	A	T	■	R	E	H	O	A	■	D	I	M	■
A	E	I	O	■	I	S	E	R	E	■	O	R	A	S
C	A	R	M	I	C	H	A	E	L	■	N	E	T	I
E	R	S	■	D	E	E	D	■	F	R	A	S	E	R
■	■	A	I	■	R	■	O	R	A	L	■	■	■	■
M	A	S	C	O	T	■	■	R	I	D	D	E	L	L
A	L	E	R	T	■	M	E	C	C	A	■	D	O	E
R	I	P	E	■	E	M	U	■	■	■	Y	E	G	G
E	C	T	■	H	U	G	O	S	■	C	O	M	A	E
S	E	S	T	I	N	A	■	■	P	E	K	A	N	S
■	■	E	L	A	N	■	C	■	L	E	■	■	■	■
S	T	E	L	L	I	■	E	R	A	L	■	M	O	N
H	E	L	L	■	D	E	V	O	N	S	H	I	R	E
E	D	I	E	■	E	L	E	M	I	■	U	S	E	S
■	A	A	R	■	D	Y	N	E	S	■	M	E	L	T

Cards on the Table   14

R	H	O	D	A		D	Y	E	D		B	O	D	Y
A	E	G	I	R		R	A	C	E		A	B	I	E
L	L		P	I		A	R	G	E	N	T	I	N	A
P	G	A		A	C	I	D		R	A	T	T	E	R
H	A	M	A	D	A	N		G	I	R	L			
			I	N	N		D	A	N	C	E	R	S	
S	E	C	R	E	T		E	R	G	O		A	C	E
A	L	E	S			A	V	E		A	M	A	R	
O	B	E		A	D	M	I		A	D	M	I	R	E
	A	S	T	W	E	L	L		G	A	E			
		E	A	S	E		R	U	S	S	I	A	N	
C	A	T	N	I	P		S	U	E	T		U	P	I
A	D	A	P	T	A	B	L	E		A	D		P	G
S	A	K	I		R	O	A	R		R	U	B	L	E
E	D	E	N		D	O	M	S		D	O	V	E	R

Death on the Nile   16

L	S	D		D	A	R	T	H		M	E	N	A
A	T	E	N		I	P		I	O		A	L	I	F
S	I	M	O	N	D	O	Y	L	E		R	E	L	Y
	R	E	V	E	N	G	E		R	I	V	E	R
		E	T	T	E		W	O	D	E		
F	O	O	L		E	G	Y	P	T		G	L	C
L	A	T	I	N		L	E	U		S		E	O
E	T	E	S		S	W	I	S	S		C	L	E	O
A	E		T		I	U	D		T	H	I	C	K
S	S	T		A	Z	T	E	C		U	G	H	S
		T	R	E	E		L	A	D	Y		
H	E	A	R	T		R	O	S	A	L	I	E
E	D	G	E		T	O	A	S	T	M	E	L	B	A
A	N	N	A		I	V		E	R		R	I	O	T
D	A	I	S		M	O	T	T	O		A	N	E

D	A	C	H	A		A	C	T	S		A	N	T	S
E	L	L	I	S		S	O	H	O		R	E	E	L
E	D	I	T	H		T	R	U	E		T	A	R	A
R	A	P		E	W	I	N	G		F	I	R	S	T
		P	S	I		I		M	I	S	S	E	S	
E	S	A	U		M	R	S	H	A	R	T			
M	I	D	R	I	B		H	A	R	M		A	J	A
M	A	D	I	S	O	N		H	I	L	L	M	A	N
A	M	A		A	R	I	L		T	Y	P	I	N	G
		S	A	N	D	E	R	S		G	L	E	E	
T	H	R	I	C	E		O		K	R	A			
R	E	A	L	S		A	N	G	I	O		A	G	A
A	N	D	A		J	E	A	N		B	A	C	O	N
D	R	A	G		A	R	R	A		B	R	Y	A	N
E	Y	R	E		H	Y	D	R		Y	A	L	T	A

Nemesis   24

L	O	V	E		A	S	P	S		E	S	C	A
I	N	E	E		S	T	O	P		A	L	T	O	N
B	E	R	G		G	O	L	A		B	L	A	C	K
R	I	I		J	A	S	O	N		S	A	R	A	H
A	R	T	H	U	R	S		B	O	S			
	Y	O	N	D		D	O	O	R		C	B	I
S	C	H	M	O		N	O	R	A	B	R	O	A	D
T	R	U	E		P	O	L	A	R		O	N	T	O
E	A	N	D	E	R	S	O	N		D	U	C	A	L
T	N	T		P	O	U	R		T	U	T	U	
		S	R	A		N	E	M	E	S	I	S	
R	E	C	T	I		E	T	Y	M	A		S	O	L
I	L	I	A	C		S	A	L	P		T	I	N	A
C	O	O	K	E		T	O	O	L		J	O	A	N
E	N	N	E		E	S	N	E		I	N	S	T

105

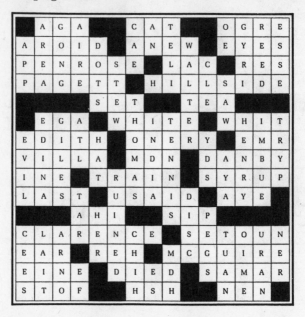

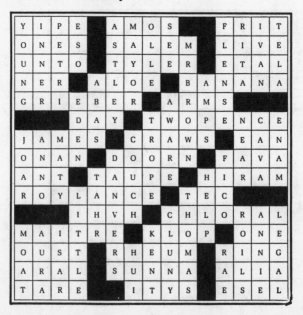

F	E	B	S		A	D	A	M			S	A	N	S
I	D	E	O		S	E	R	E	D		I	N	E	E
F	I	T	S		P	R	I	M	E		G	A	R	N
T	N	T		T	E	E	D		B	I	N	I	O	N
H	A	Y	D	O	C	K		D	O	R	A			
		A	N	T		W	I	R	E	L	E	S	S	
T	O	M	M	Y		N	I	S	A	N		T	O	P
A	L	A	E		L	A	R	C	H		A	N	N	A
M	E	A		B	U	R	R	S		B	R	A	G	S
P	A	T	R	I	C	I	A		C	A	R			
		E	R	I	S		F	A	R	A	D	A	Y	
B	E	H	A	L	F		E	R	R	S		A	G	E
A	V	E	C		E	L	D	E	R		E	N	N	A
T	O	R	T		R	O	N	D	O		I	C	E	S
T	E	A	S		K	A	A	T		R	E	S	T	

By the Pricking of My Thumbs   32

E	M	M	A		A	G	U	E	S		P	R	O	P
M	E	A	D		F	U	N	G	I		H	A	L	T
I	R	R	A		R	I	D	G	E		I	N	I	A
T	U	I		L	I	L	Y		B	L	I	G	H	
	A	L	I	C	E		A	L	A	I				
C	C		O	V	A		S	C	U	L	P	T	O	R
H	O	U	S	E		S	P	O	C	K		E	R	E
A	C	N	E		P	E	R	R	Y		B	A	D	E
M	O	C		S	L	A	I	N		T	I	M	E	D
P	A	I	N	T	I	N	G		C	A	R		R	S
		E	Y	E	S		M	O	O	D	Y			
B	O	R	A	X		S	O	W	S		O	R	P	
O	M	E	R		C	A	N	A	L		D	R	E	I
A	R	A	L		U	N	I	T	E		A	K	I	N
T	I	D	Y		P	A	T	S	Y		D	E	S	K

Postern of Fate 34

B	A	B	S	■	M	A	B	E	L	■	K	A	N	E
A	G	E	E	■	U	R	A	T	E	■	A	B	E	L
C	A	R	R	O	T	Y	T	O	M	■	I	R	I	S
H	O	T	■	S	T	A	T	■	■	S	K	A	T	E
■	■	E	L	O	N	■	P	O	O	A	■	■	■	■
L	U	P	T	O	N	■	H	A	N	N	I	B	A	L
A	N	A	T	■	■	M	O	L	L	Y	■	I	N	O
N	A	P	E	■	B	A	R	M	Y	■	A	R	G	O
A	P	A	■	T	O	R	S	I	■	■	C	L	U	B
I	T	W	A	S	O	N	E	■	P	R	I	S	S	Y
■	■	N	I	K	E	■	P	A	I	D	■	■	■	■
P	A	N	D	A	■	B	A	L	M	■	N	A	T	■
A	R	A	R	■	T	H	E	L	A	U	R	E	L	S
V	A	S	E	■	I	S	A	A	C	■	E	S	A	U
E	N	O	W	■	T	H	R	E	E	■	S	T	E	N

The Pale Horse 36

W	A	R	M	■	M	O	G	U	L	■	G	R	E	Y
E	L	I	A	■	A	R	E	T	E	■	R	U	N	E
B	A	E	R	■	C	A	L	E	S	■	I	B	I	T
B	E	N	T	H	A	L	L	■	S	A	M	E	D	I
■	■	I	O	N	S	■	H	O	B	O	■	■	■	■
B	E	A	N	E	D	■	C	O	R	R	I	G	A	N
E	M	S	■	D	A	V	I	S	■	A	R	O	S	E
L	E	K	S	■	L	A	N	E	S	■	E	R	S	E
L	E	E	T	S	■	U	D	D	E	R	■	S	O	D
A	R	D	I	N	G	L	Y	■	R	A	V	E	N	S
■	■	R	Y	O	T	■	A	G	I	O	■	■	■	■
C	A	L	L	E	R	■	T	H	E	D	O	S	S	U
A	L	I	I	■	M	A	R	I	A	■	D	E	E	R
I	D	E	N	■	A	L	I	G	N	■	O	R	B	S
D	O	U	G	■	N	I	G	H	T	■	O	B	I	A

Hallowe'en Party   38

S	O	F	A		E	R	R	S		A	P	A	P
O	M	I	T		D	R	E	A	D		D	E	M	I
J	A	N	E	T	W	H	I	T	E		V	E	I	N
A	N	N		H	I	E	S		S	P	E	N	C	E
		T	I	N	A		Y	M	E	R		
R	O	W	E	N	A		G	O	O	D	B	O	D	Y
A	P	H	I	S		M	A	G	N	I		K	A	O
K	I	E	L		L	I	N	E	D		P	A	T	U
E	N	L		R	E	F	E	E		J	A	P	E	S
S	E	M	I	N	O	F	F		L	O	U	I	S	E
		N	A	P	S		T	E	Y	L	
G	L	O	S	S	O		B	O	S	C		E	S	O
O	A	S	T		L	E	A	D	B	E	T	T	E	R
B	R	E	A		D	A	V	A	O		I	T	E	A
Y	A	R	R		R	E	Y	S		W	E	L	L

Elephants Can Remember   40

A	M	A	S		S	A	R	A		P	E	L	F
V	I	L	E		E	R	A	T	O		O	L	O	R
I	N	I	A		C	E	C	I	L		I	O	N	E
L	O	B		I	O	T	A		D	A	R	N	E	D
A	R	I	A	D	N	E		E	S	S	O		
	R	E	D		A	L	I	S	T	A	I	R
G	R	E	E	N		G	R	A	N	T		P	G	A
R	A	M	S		M	I	M	E	S		T	A	N	S
A	M	I		P	A	L	E	O		M	A	R	I	A
M	A	R	G	A	R	E	T		B	A	L	
	N	I	L	S		S	U	I	C	I	D	E
B	E	F	O	R	E		S	I	N	D		L	O	A
O	R	E	S		N	A	N	N	Y		C	E	L	T
O	M	N	I		E	R	I	C	A		P	A	L	O
M	A	N	S		O	P	E	N		L	Ł	Y	N

The Secret of Chimneys   42

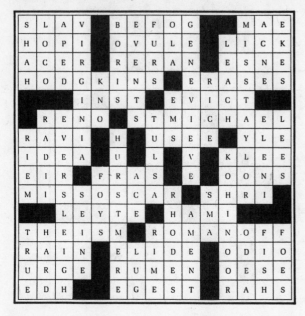

The Man in the Brown Suit   44

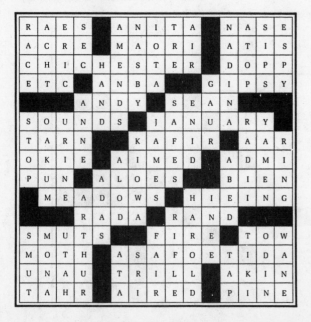

Crooked House 46

S	O	J	A	░	P	H	A	N	E	░	B	A	W	L
O	D	O	R	░	H	O	R	A	L	░	A	L	E	E
D	E	H	A	V	I	L	A	N	D	░	L	I	S	T
A	R	N	░	L	E	D	░	░	F	L	A	T	░	░
░	░	S	A	I	D	░	B	R	I	E	░	░	░	░
T	R	A	N	S	P	░	A	R	I	S	T	I	D	E
H	A	L	E	S	░	T	R	O	T	H	░	M	E	G
R	I	B	E	░	C	R	E	W	E	░	K	A	N	E
E	N	E	░	G	R	O	A	N	░	M	A	G	D	A
E	Y	E	D	R	O	P	S	░	G	O	V	E	R	N
░	░	R	A	C	E	░	J	A	T	I	░	░	░	░
░	B	H	O	Y	░	C	A	B	░	░	T	R	Y	░
T	O	O	N	░	S	W	I	N	L	Y	D	E	A	N
R	O	W	E	░	A	I	M	E	E	░	U	S	M	C
E	K	E	S	░	G	N	A	T	S	░	I	T	E	A

Endless Night 48

B	A	F	F	░	L	I	D	O	░	░	L	E	E	░
A	C	R	E	░	A	M	O	R	E	░	H	I	V	E
S	H	A	W	░	W	I	L	D	S	░	O	V	E	N
T	E	N	░	D	Y	N	A	░	T	O	W	E	R	S
░	░	K	O	R	E	A	░	C	H	E	E	R	░	░
░	F	░	S	E	R	░	H	U	E	S	░	F	B	░
H	O	R	S	E	░	T	E	R	R	E	░	O	R	O
A	L	A	I	░	I	N	S	░	░	A	T	E	N	░
F	L	Y	░	S	N	A	R	E	░	L	L	O	Y	D
T	Y	░	M	A	R	Y	░	R	O	E	░	A	░	░
░	G	R	E	T	A	░	V	O	I	C	E	░	░	░
M	I	L	I	E	U	░	M	I	G	S	░	L	A	B
I	S	I	S	░	R	E	E	C	E	░	B	L	U	E
K	A	N	E	░	E	L	G	A	R	░	V	I	N	E
E	R	T	░	░	M	A	R	S	░	M	E	E	T	░

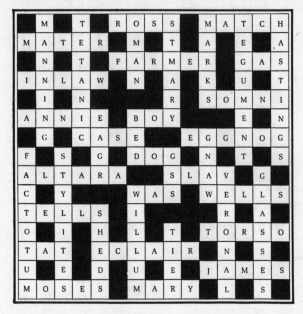

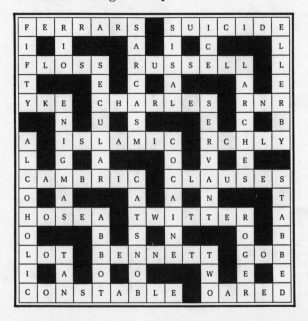

```
C H A R L E S     M A N D E R S
Y       A   C       E       N     P
    C A M B E L L     J U D G E     E
T     A       N     F     O             I
H I D     P E T R O C H       S I R
I     O     A     R     N     T
A R G O S     A R T I S T E       D
      A     S     L     O     P     R
R A N D A L L     C Y N T H I A
I         G     U     H       E       M
V     F R E D D I E     R A N I A
I     A         E     L     O       T
E A U     I N S I S T S       O B I
R     S     S     E     E     D S
A C T O R     A M A S S M E N T
```

```
    G R E E N     W I N D B A G
    E       V     E     A         N
A L I B I     P I L A R     C U P
L         L H I     O     E     O     I
F     D         J E N N I F E R     G
R E E V E S         D     U     S
E     S         C O R S I C A
D     D     S     A     N     E     A
    H E R C U L E         A     R
B     M     R     F     L O C K E T
R     O V E R R I P E     E     I
A     N     A     E     P E G     S
T E A     M E D I C     R O A S T
    V         R     N     A     E
    E N G L A N D     L Y D I A
```

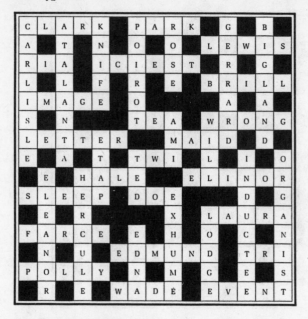

```
C O R N C R A K E     D E   M O B
H   I   O   C         I   I       R
O R B   C O T T A G E     D C I
C       O   R   L         G     T
O S T I A   E F F A B L E     I
L   O       S   R   A           S
A R T I S T S   E N G L I S H
T   E   E       G   H   N
E   M I R A C L E   D O R I S
    I   V   R       A   O   I
E T C   I R E L A N D   A I M
L       C   V   U       D   N
S T O V E   I S L A N D S   O
I   B       C   I   E       N
E B B T I D E   C O O M B E S
```

```
F E L I C I T Y   H   L   L
I   T   I   H   V A L E R I E
J O H N S T O N   L   M   L
I       S   M   A L T O S A X
S A L L Y   A C M E   N   C
    E       S   B       S   R
S H E I L A   H O T   S H O E
I   W       L   U   W       R   N
L E A R   I V E   O N E E L E
K   Y       E   U       W
    M   C   I R I S   I N D I A
S A B R I N A   E   R       L
    R   I   A   A F F E C T E D
D I A M O N D   U   N   R   E
    A   E   E   A L G E R I A N
```

The Clocks   66

The Moving Finger   68

A Murder is Announced 70

```
. . A D J U S T . . P E A .
D . P I P . O . W . H U E . A
E . . T O A D E L I . A . . C
A C R E . N . T . N O R T H
T . E . M A . A T I C . L . I
H A V O C . C . E . H A S T E
. D . C O L O N E L . . U
R O Y A L . I . H . I T A L Y
. L . E A T H A L F . . L
O F F A L . H . M . F U S E D
B . Y . L E E R . L E . P . I
J U L I A . R . D . M A M A
E . F . N A I R O B I . . N
C . O L D . N . R . S I R . A
T O T . I G U A N A
```

A Pocket Full of Rye 72

```
R U B Y . I D E A . S E B U M
E . R . E . A . L . L . R . E
P N E U M O N I A . A D E L E
P . D . P . E . S . N . A . K
U R A N I U M . K O D A K S .
. . . R . E . A . E . F . S
S A N D E M A N . U R B A N E
O . A . . D . A . . . S . X
N O R W A Y . I D O L A T R Y
G . C . S . I . U . O
. V I V I A N . L E N S C A P
P . S . A . S . T . D . A . I
R E S E T . A D E N O I D A L
I . U . I . N . R . N . R . O
M U S I C . E N Y A . B E R T
```

```
A R T H U R . . . N Y M P H
L . . A . E . K I N O . A . E
F . S T R A I N . . I . R . A
R A T . I . I . A R T I S T
E . M . B R I G G S . . N . H
D I A N E . . H . P . D A M E
. R . A . E T L I D O . . R
. H Y A D E S . . R . C . W
. A . . L . T . H E S T I A
. L . F E M A L E . . O . T
E L L A . . T . A . A R G U S
D . . R . A E O L U S . . S
D E R M O T . . T . T . L I L
I . . E . L . C H E R R Y . E
E N T R A I L . . . O . E O N
```

Caribbean Mystery   76

```
. . J O A N . C A B L E S .
T W O . . I . R . . T I M
O . E C C E N T R I C . O . O
R . . A . M . . D . A . L
Q . K E N D A L . E . I T A L
U R N . A . T . S P A . . Y
A . I N D I E S . A N D
Y L F . I . . E . L . I R E
. E R A . E N I G M A . V
S . . O N E . . O . R . N A I
C R E E . D . A R M A D A . L
A . L . W . . E . V . . E
R . L . C A R I B B E A N . Y
F R I . R . . O . . E Y E
. S H A D O W . P O N D .
```

The Seven Dials Mystery   80

TITLES

1 THE ABC MURDERS
2 AT BERTRAM'S HOTEL
3 THE BIG FOUR
4 THE BOOMERANG CLUE
5 CARDS ON THE TABLE
6 A CARIBBEAN MYSTERY
7 CAT AMONG THE PIGEONS
8 THE CLOCKS
9 CROOKED HOUSE
10 CURTAIN
11 DEAD MAN'S FOLLY
12 DEATH IN THE CLOUDS
13 DEATH ON THE NILE
14 DESTINATION UNKNOWN
15 DOUBLE SIN
16 DUMB WITNESS
17 ENDLESS NIGHT
18 THE GOLDEN BALL
19 HALLOWE'EN PARTY
20 HICKORY, DICKORY, DOCK
21 A HOLIDAY FOR MURDER
22 THE HOLLOW
23 HOUND OF DEATH
24 THE MOUSETRAP
25 MURDER AT THE VICARAGE

26 MURDER IN MESOPOTAMIA
27 MURDER IN THREE ACTS
28 MURDER IS EASY
29 MURDER ON THE LINKS
30 MURDER SHE SAID
31 THE MYSTERIOUS AFFAIR AT STYLES
32 NEMESIS
33 N OR M?
34 ONE, TWO, BUCKLE MY SHOE
35 ORDEAL BY INNOCENCE
36 THE PALE HORSE
37 PASSENGER TO FRANKFURT
38 PERIL AT END HOUSE
39 POSTERN OF FATE
40 REMEMBERED DEATH
41 THE SECRET ADVERSARY
42 THE SECRET OF CHIMNEYS
43 THE SEVEN DIALS MYSTERY
44 THE SITTAFORD MYSTERY
45 SLEEPING MURDER
46 TEN LITTLE INDIANS
47 THERE IS A TIDE
48 THIRD GIRL
49 TOWARDS ZERO
50 THE UNDER DOG

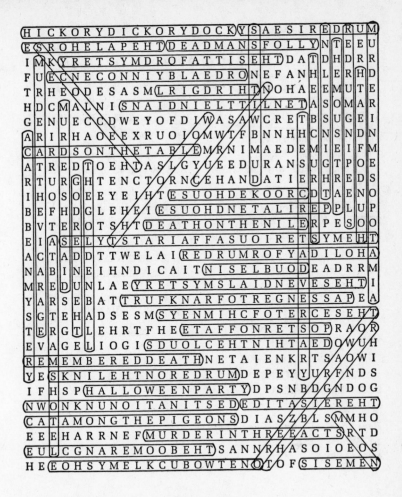

QUOTATION

HEIGHT FIVE FEET FOUR INCHES, EGG-SHAPED HEAD CARRIED A
LITTLE TO ONE SIDE, EYES THAT SHONE GREEN WHEN HE WAS
EXCITED, STIFF MILITARY MOUSTACHE, AIR OF DIGNITY IMMENSE!
HE WAS NEAT AND DANDIFIED IN APPEARANCE. FOR NEATNESS OF
ANY KIND HE HAD AN ABSOLUTE PASSION. . . .ORDER AND METHOD
WERE HIS GODS.

CLUE ANSWERS

1 HERCULE POIROT
2 ARTHUR HASTINGS
3 MURDER ON THE LINKS

CLUE ANSWERS

The Middle-Aged Wife
1 NANCY, 2 MARIA PACKINGTON,
3 GEORGE PACKINGTON

The Discontented Soldier
1 FREDA CLEGG, 2 JERRY,
3 OLIVER, 4 PERCY, 5 WILBRAHAM

The Distressed Lady
1 NAOMI DORTHEIMER,
2 REUBEN, 3 JULES, 4 ERNESTINE,
5 SANCHIA, 6 DAPHNE

The Discontented Husband
1 MASSINGTON, 2 IRIS,
3 REGINALD WADE

The City Clerk
1 LUCAS, 2 OLGA, 3 ROBERTS,
4 MAGGIE SAYERS, 5 PAUL

The Rich Woman
1 ANTROBUS, 2 C. CONSTANTINE,
3 GARDNER, 4 HANNAH,
5 RYMER, 6 JOE

Have You Got Everything You Want?
1 EDWARD, 2 ELSIE, 3 JEFFRIES,
4 SUBAYSKA

The Gate of Bagdad
1 POLI, 2 PRYCE, 3 NETTA,
4 LONG, 5 HENSLEY, 6 LOFTUS,
7 PENTEMIAN

The House at Shiraz
1 CARR, 2 KING, 3 SCHLAGAL

The Pearl of Price
1 CALEB, 2 CAROL, 3 CARVER,
4 DUBOSC, 5 JIM, 6 MARVEL

Death on the Nile
1 GEORGE, 2 WEST, 3 GRAYLE,
4 ELSIE, 5 MOHAMMED

The Oracle at Delphi
1 PETERS, 2 WILLARD JR.

Names Appearing in Several Stories
1 MISS LEMON, 2 MADELEINE DE
SARA, 3 CLAUDE LUTTRELL,
4 MR. PARKER, 5 PYNE

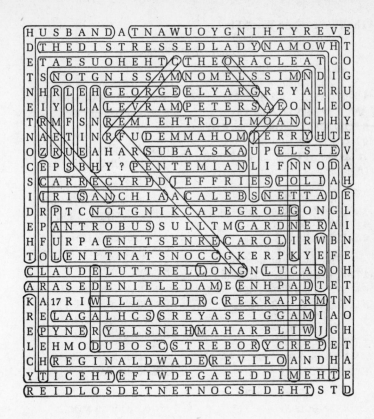

ADVERTISEMENT

ARE YOU HAPPY? IF NOT, CONSULT MR. PARKER PYNE, 17 RICHMOND ST.

CLUE ANSWERS

The Harlequin Tea Set
1 THOMAS, 2 ALI, 3 HARLEY BARLEY, 4 BERYL, 5 LILY, 6 ROLAND, 7 SIMON, 8 TIMOTHY, 9 DR. HORTON, 10 INEZ, 11 MARIA, 12 HERMES, 13 HARLEY QUIN

The Coming of Mr. Quin
1 RICHARD, 2 LAURA, 3 ALEC, 4 ELEANOR, 5 TOM, 6 SATTERTHWAITE

The Shadow on the Glass
1 JIMMY, 2 DRAGE, 3 PORTER, 4 MOIRA, 5 SCOTT, 6 IRIS, 7 NED, 8 UNKERTON, 9 WINKFIELD

At The Bells and Motley
1 WILLIAM, 2 ELEANOR, 3 MATHIAS, 4 HARWELL, 5 MARY JONES

The Sign in the Sky
1 LOUISA BULLARD, 2 SYLVIA DALE, 3 DENMAN, 4 MARTIN

The Soul of the Croupier
1 ELIZABETH, 2 MIRABELLE, 3 RUDGE, 4 JEANNE, 5 PIERRE

The World's End
1 NAOMI, 2 GERARD, 3 JUDD, 4 NUNN, 5 TOMLINSON, 6 VYSE

The Voice in the Dark
1 BARRON, 2 BIMBO, 3 ALICE, 4 GALE, 5 MARCIA, 6 LLOYD, 7 ROLEY, 8 BABS

The Face of Helen
1 BURNS, 2 PHIL, 3 WEST

The Dead Harlequin
1 FRANK, 2 ALIX, 3 COBB, 4 FORD, 5 GLEN, 6 LADY

The Bird with the Broken Wing
1 MABELLE, 2 DORIS, 3 JOHN, 4 ADA, 5 MADGE, 6 SARAH, 7 ANNESLEY

The Man from the Sea
1 CODSON, 2 PAZ

Harlequin's Lane
1 ANN, 2 JOHN, 3 MOLLY

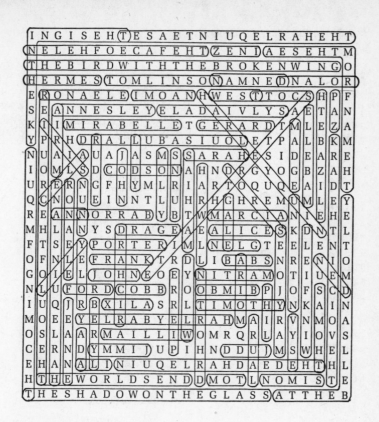

TITLES

THE PASSING OF MR. QUIN
THE MYSTERIOUS MR. QUIN

3 Letters

1 OLD

4 Letters

1 ANNE
2 CRAM
3 HILL
4 MARY
5 ROSE

5 Letters

1 ADAMS
2 CLARA
3 HAWES
4 PRICE
5 SLACK
6 STONE
7 VICAR

6 Letters

1 AMANDA
2 ARCHER
3 DENNIS
4 GLADYS
5 LUCIUS
6 MARTHA
7 REEVES
8 RIDLEY
9 SADLER

7 Letters

1 CORONER
2 INQUEST
3 LEONARD
4 LETTICE
5 REDDING
6 ROBERTS
7 SIMMONS

8 Letters

1 CAROLINE
2 HARTNELL
3 LAWRENCE
4 MRS. PRATT
5 WETHERBY

9 Letters

1 DR. HAYDOCK
2 PROTHEROE

10 Letters

1 MUCH BENHAM
2 ST. MARY MEAD

11 Letters

1 RAYMOND WEST

12 Letters

1 MRS. LESTRANGE

14 Letters

1 MISS JANE MARPLE
2 CONSTABLE HURST

15 Letters

1 GRISELDA CLEMENT

19 Letters

1 MURDER AT THE VICARAGE

The Other Hercule Poirot Cipher 94

KEY PHRASE

ACHILLE POIROT

MESSAGE

THE MAN BESIDE ME WAS NOT HERCULE POIROT.

HE WAS VERY LIKE HIM, EXTRAORDINARILY LIKE HIM. THERE WAS THE SAME EGG-SHAPED HEAD, THE SAME STRUTTING FIGURE, DELICATELY PLUMP. BUT THE VOICE WAS DIFFERENT, AND THE EYES INSTEAD OF BEING GREEN WERE DARK, AND SURELY THE MOUSTACHES — THOSE FAMOUS MOUSTACHES —?

MY RELFECTIONS WERE CUT SHORT BY THE COUNTESS'S VOICE. SHE STEPPED FORWARD, HER VOICE RINGING WITH EXCITEMENT. "YOU HAVE BEEN DECEIVED. THAT MAN IS NOT HERCULE POIROT!"

The Miss Marple Quotefall   99

QUOTATION

YOU SIMPLY CANNOT AFFORD TO BELIEVE EVERYTHING THAT PEOPLE TELL YOU. WHEN THERE'S ANYTHING FISHY ABOUT, I NEVER BELIEVE ANYONE AT ALL. YOU SEE, I KNOW HUMAN NATURE SO WELL. MISS JANE MARPLE

SOURCE

THE BODY IN THE LIBRARY

The Poisoner's Word Grid & Match-up 96

VICTIM	POISONS	MEANS	BOOK
AMYAS CRALE	HEMLOCK	BEER	MURDER IN RETROSPECT (FIVE LITTLE PIGS)
HAROLD CRACKENTHORPE	ACONITE	TABLETS	WHAT MRS. MCGILLICUDDY SAW! (4:50 FROM PADDINGTON)
ALFRED CRACKENTHORPE	ARSENIC	TEA	WHAT MRS. MCGILLICUDDY SAW! (4:50 FROM PADDINGTON)
ARISTIDE LEONIDES	ESERINE	INSULIN	CROOKED HOUSE
GERRY WADE	CHLORAL	WHISKY	THE SEVEN DIALS MYSTERY
GEORGE BARTON	CYANIDE	WINE	REMEMBERED DEATH (SPARKLING CYANIDE)
MRS. FERRARS	VERONAL	SUICIDE	THE MURDER OF ROGER ACKROYD
ELLA ZIELINSKY	PRUSSIC	ATOMIZER	THE MIRROR CRACK'D FROM SIDE TO SIDE
CHARLES CRADDOCK	ANTHRAX	SHAVING BRUSH	CARDS ON THE TABLE
COCO COURTENEY	COCAINE	OVERDOSE	"THE AFFAIR AT THE VICTORY BALL"
MARY GERRARD	MORPHIA	SANDWICH	SAD CYPRESS

The Case of the Noted Nephew: An Agatha Christie Double Crostic   100

A $\frac{N}{13}$ $\frac{E}{23}$ $\frac{O}{60}$ $\frac{T}{69}$ $\frac{E}{81}$ $\frac{N}{88}$ $\frac{I}{107}$ $\frac{C}{15}$

B $\frac{O}{63}$ $\frac{B}{74}$ $\frac{L}{90}$ $\frac{A}{92}$ $\frac{T}{96}$ $\frac{E}{98}$

C $\frac{V}{112}$ $\frac{E}{113}$ $\frac{S}{114}$ $\frac{S}{117}$ $\frac{E}{132}$ $\frac{L}{21}$

D $\frac{E}{26}$ $\frac{A}{79}$ $\frac{S}{93}$ $\frac{E}{102}$ $\frac{L}{103}$ $\frac{S}{122}$

E $\frac{L}{129}$ $\frac{O}{5}$ $\frac{B}{43}$ $\frac{B}{83}$ $\frac{I}{111}$ $\frac{E}{6}$ $\frac{D}{64}$

F $\frac{I}{68}$ $\frac{N}{95}$ $\frac{S}{123}$ $\frac{U}{128}$ $\frac{L}{130}$ $\frac{I}{2}$ $\frac{N}{30}$

G $\frac{S}{41}$ $\frac{H}{51}$ $\frac{I}{72}$ $\frac{F}{116}$ $\frac{T}{19}$ $\frac{L}{22}$ $\frac{E}{33}$ $\frac{S}{54}$ $\frac{S}{55}$

H $\frac{T}{86}$ $\frac{E}{91}$ $\frac{E}{104}$ $\frac{N}{108}$ $\frac{A}{121}$ $\frac{G}{126}$ $\frac{E}{12}$

I $\frac{R}{27}$ $\frac{A}{82}$ $\frac{V}{11}$ $\frac{I}{18}$ $\frac{S}{28}$ $\frac{H}{32}$ $\frac{E}{44}$ $\frac{S}{73}$

J $\frac{A}{94}$ $\frac{M}{7}$ $\frac{P}{17}$ $\frac{L}{45}$ $\frac{I}{46}$ $\frac{F}{61}$ $\frac{I}{124}$ $\frac{E}{47}$ $\frac{S}{78}$

K $\frac{Y}{70}$ $\frac{U}{85}$ $\frac{K}{77}$ $\frac{O}{84}$ $\frac{N}{125}$

L $\frac{M}{34}$ $\frac{O}{75}$ $\frac{O}{76}$ $\frac{L}{101}$ $\frac{A}{105}$

M $\frac{O}{115}$ $\frac{C}{38}$ $\frac{C}{58}$ $\frac{U}{87}$ $\frac{P}{89}$ $\frac{I}{29}$ $\frac{E}{49}$ $\frac{D}{106}$

N $\frac{N}{131}$ $\frac{A}{10}$ $\frac{P}{97}$ $\frac{H}{1}$ $\frac{T}{24}$ $\frac{H}{36}$ $\frac{A}{16}$

O $\frac{D}{127}$ $\frac{E}{52}$ $\frac{A}{20}$ $\frac{R}{66}$ $\frac{T}{25}$ $\frac{H}{39}$ $\frac{S}{133}$

P $\frac{W}{35}$ $\frac{H}{71}$ $\frac{I}{37}$ $\frac{L}{110}$ $\frac{O}{14}$ $\frac{M}{62}$

Q $\frac{E}{65}$ $\frac{V}{48}$ $\frac{E}{53}$ $\frac{N}{57}$ $\frac{I}{40}$ $\frac{N}{67}$ $\frac{G}{109}$

R $\frac{S}{134}$ $\frac{U}{118}$ $\frac{P}{120}$ $\frac{P}{4}$ $\frac{O}{99}$ $\frac{R}{119}$ $\frac{T}{31}$ $\frac{E}{59}$ $\frac{R}{80}$

S $\frac{T}{50}$ $\frac{H}{9}$ $\frac{E}{56}$ $\frac{S}{3}$ $\frac{P}{100}$ $\frac{I}{42}$ $\frac{S}{8}$

Acrostic puzzle grid:

1 N H	2 F I	3 S S		4 R P	5 E O	6 E E	7 J M	8 S S				
9 S H	10 N A	11 I V	12 H E		13 A N	14 P O		15 A C	16 N A	17 J P	18 I I	19 G T	20 O A	21 C L
	22 G L	23 A E	24 N T	25 O T	26 D E	27 I R	28 I S		29 M I	30 F N		31 R T	32 I H	33 G E
34 L M		35 P W	36 N H	37 P I	38 M C	39 O H		40 Q I	41 G S		42 S I		43 E B	44 I E
45 J L	46 J I	47 J E	48 Q V	49 M E		50 S T	51 G H	52 O E		53 Q E	54 G S	55 G S	56 S E	57 Q N
58 M C	59 R E		60 A O	61 J F		62 P M	63 B O	64 E D	65 Q E	66 O R	67 Q N	68 F I	69 A T	70 K Y
	71 P H	72 G I	73 I S		74 B B	75 L O	76 L O	77 K K	78 J S		79 D A	80 R R	81 A E	
82 I A	83 E B	84 K O	85 K U	86 H T		87 M U	88 A N	89 M P	90 B L	91 H E	92 B A	93 D S	94 J A	95 F N
96 B T		97 N P	98 B E	99 R O	100 S P	101 L L	102 D E		103 D L	104 H E	105 L A	106 M D	107 A I	108 H N
109 Q G		110 P L	111 E I	112 C V	113 C E	114 C S		115 M O	116 G F		117 C S	118 R U	119 R R	120 R P
121 H A	122 D S	123 F S	124 J I	125 K N	126 H G		127 O D	128 F U	129 E L	130 H L	131 N N	132 C E	133 O S	134 R S